OXFORD LIFE IN THE TWENTIETH CENTURY

Oxford Life in the Twentieth Century

Agnes Florence (Clarice) Wood BEM

Carnegie Publishing Ltd

Published in 2003 by Carnegie Publishing Ltd
Carnegie House, Chatsworth Road
Lancaster LAI 4SL
publishing website: www.carnegiepub.co.uk
book production website: www.wooof.net

British Library Cataloguing-in-Publication data
A catalogue record for this book is available from the British Library

ISBN 1-85936-090-4

Typeset in Adobe Garamond by Carnegie Publishing
Printed and bound in the UK by
Biddles Ltd, Guildford and King's Lynn

Contents

To be interested in what you are doing is the surest way to success and enjoyment

I

Childhood

MEADOW LANE, Iffley, Oxford, although little better than a mud track, was to me as a child one of the most beautiful places in the world. For it was here on 13 February 1901 that I was born and spent the first twenty-one years of my life.

The great blessings I enjoyed were found amidst the peace and beauty of the countryside.

I recall the water meadows stretching down to the river Thames, the brightly coloured horse-drawn coal barges and houseboats, and the Eights that started just below on the Isis. I remember the hot scorching sun that followed a torrential downpour when the ground would steam and the lane would come alive with hundreds of small frogs that had just emerged from their tadpole stage in the nearby brook. This seasonable exodus was well known and although there was never much around, carters would pull up their horses and people would wait until they had all managed to either hop or crawl across the lane to the safety of the fields beyond.

I have happy memories of the early morning dew, the babbling brook, the birds' song and the bats that darted to and fro in the evening twilight. At night time stars twinkled from a clear night sky. There were no street lamps to mar their beauty, the only light coming from an occasional star shooting across the sky.

In the distance could be seen the lights of Oxford, dimly showing the outlines of the city's towers and spires. When the wind was in the right direction I could hear the bell in Tom Tower striking its one hundred and one notes. It all seemed so far away, as indeed it was, Iffley village being some two miles from the city centre. In 1928 it became a suburb of Oxford.

Before this, Iffley was quite unspoilt. I remember the terraced houses that stood amidst the more gracious splendour of the larger houses with their winding drives, lawns and beautiful flower beds and Box Cottage with its overhanging shrubs and creepers that one had to battle through to reach the front door. I recall the walled stone built cottages where lived the Duffields and Carpenters.

At the entrance to Tree Lane was a mound on which grew a large elm tree. Its huge trunk provided us children with a good game of hide and seek. It was near here that the village Stocks had stood. These had existed between the years 1860 and 1870. A beautiful old world thatched cottage marked the entrance to Mill Lane, whilst further along the old Mill House and water mill could be seen nestling supremely among the tall poplar trees. By the side was a small field with a watering place adjoining, where, as a child, I used to paddle and riders brought their horses down for a swim.

The twisting lane led onwards past the Rectory to the twelfth century Norman Church of St Mary the Virgin standing in its walled churchyard, the entrance to the churchyard being marked by a large chestnut tree, which when in blossom was an unforgettable sight. Near here stood the old thatched school. Built in 1828 it existed until its closure in 1961.

Beyond the churchyard was a right-of-way that led up the hill to the village of Littlemore. Primroses grew in a grove by the hillside, whilst along the hedgerow could be seen clumps of white violets. Fields of golden corn stretched out as far as the eye could see. Above, the skylark soared, its lovely song contrasting strangely with the rasping note of the corncrake in the fields below.

The village boasted two pubs, the *Tree Hotel* and the *Prince of Wales*. It had a butcher's shop and two general shops and these, together with the bakery and a sub-post office, completed the commercial side.

Iffley had a mixed community made up of the rich, poor and middle class. Friendship, if any, was only to be found with relatives or a near neighbour. Gossiping seldom extended outside the pubs or village shops, for it was a time when the gentry held the centre of influence and behaviour of this kind would have been greatly frowned upon.

Many families depended on the gentry for their livelihood and were employed as gardeners, stable-lads, and doing odd jobs in the house. Mothers were employed as part-time cooks. Daughters 'lived in' and worked as parlour maids, housemaids and scullery maids as they were called. The latter were jack of all trades and at the beck and call of all, including members of the domestic staff.

Most of the gentry attended church on a Sunday morning, when special pews were reserved for them. After the service it was usual for the villagers to go ahead of the gentry, which meant they were always in full view. My father, who was in the choir, knew of this. On his way home he liked to call in at the pub for a drink. He always managed to avoid them by staying in the vestry until he thought they had all gone. My mother, who disapproved of any kind of deceit, often said, 'You'll do this once too many, one of these days you'll be found out.'

Then, much to our amusement it happened. I remember him coming home absolutely furious. Apparently, either by accident or design, it appeared that some of the gentry had been detained in the church. When my father emerged from the vestry, he found to his horror they were following him up the churchyard path. He dared not go to the pub and had to continue walking through the village to his home. Much to mother's delight there were no more visits to the pub on a Sunday morning, and no more spoilt dinners awaiting his return.

I like to remember the church as I knew it in my childhood days when my father sang in the choir and I attended Sunday School followed by the church service at eleven.

I recall the organist, Mr Talbot. He was a man we all greatly admired. Although completely blind, his powers of perception were wonderful. My teacher, Miss Gaskin, always escorted him to the church, where she would guide him into the pew leading to the organ. Then seating himself, he would feel his watch and as the choir entered the church he would give a nod to the waiting blower and the voluntary would begin.

I loved the festivals, for it was then that the whole church would resound with music and singing as the choir, all in their newly-laundered surplices processed up the aisle on their way to the choir stalls. As my father passed by I would pause to listen to his deep bass voice and then cast my eyes on the remaining choir, followed by the vicar.

We children occupied two pews with our teacher seated on the outside. With some of the gentry sitting behind us, there was little chance of misbehaving.

I remember one incident in particular which happened during the singing of a hymn. We suddenly became aware of a large spider on the back of a lady in front of us. This started one or two of us giggling until a sharp tap from behind brought us to our senses. With our eyes still glued to the spider, we watched spellbound as it slowly began to move upwards. Then as the lady went to sit down it gathered speed and to our horror disappeared down the back of her neck. At this one of the kids let out a loud yell which brought our teacher to her feet and we were ushered from the church. Outside we tried hard to explain what had happened, but our teacher was far too angry to listen and we were all sent home. Unfortunately for me my father had, from his seat in the choir, witnessed us being escorted from the church and when he returned home wanted to know what it was all about. Although I think he saw the funny side of it, I was nevertheless sent to bed without my Sunday dinner.

During the period 1905–10 my mother occasionally helped out at the rectory. At that time the only other person employed there was a housekeeper, but as she was of advanced years, my mother used to say she needed waiting on herself. Later, when the house-keeper decided to leave, my mother was asked to go in daily.

At that time the vicar was the Revd M. Newbolt. He was young and attractive and being unmarried, was much sought after by eligible ladies in the village. Although he was well liked by his parishioners, there were some members of the congregation who thought he was too young for a parish like Iffley. However, during the four years he was with us, he proved to be a most excellent vicar. When later it became known that he had been appointed Principal of Dorchester Missionary College, those same people who had doubted his ability were some of the first to come forward and express genuine regret at his departure. Afterwards he left Dorchester and became Residentiary Canon of Chester.

Before he left the parish we school children presented him with a pair of silver candlesticks and an oak book trough. On the sides of the latter were carved shields bearing respectively the arms of St John's College and the University.

It was at this time that the Revd Newbolt approached my mother regarding his concern at the rectory being left unoccupied. Would it be possible, he asked, for her and the family to come and live in at the vicarage until a new vicar could be installed? I was nine years old at the time and to have the opportunity of living at the rectory and, at the same time, be near the church and my school, was beyond my wildest dreams. I remember when we moved in just two days before the vicar left how on each of the evenings he gave my sister and me prayers before going to bed. I was delighted when later I was to explore the rectory house which was adjoining the churchyard on the north-west. I recall the long passages leading to two different stairways. Although it had many rooms, few showed signs of having been used for some time, for, as I opened the various doors I was to find blinds pulled down and furniture covered over with dust sheets. It all presented a very dismal sight.

The vestry at that time formed part of the rectory, and it was from here that the choir assembled to don their cassocks and surplices before walking the short distance across to the church. My greatest interest was in the south-east portion which was much earlier. Here I discovered a peculiar Buttery Hatch divided by a rather beautiful ornamental pillar of stone. For some unknown reason this area had an eerie effect on me. I would be drawn back to it time and again, always with the same feeling that I was never alone. When I mentioned this to my mother, she told me it had been used by the monks. She, herself, would never go near it. It was not until later that she told me the rectory was supposed to be haunted. If this was so, then I feel sure it must have been in this particular part.

I loved the vicarage garden with its marvellous old mulberry tree standing in the centre of the lawn and the terraced garden overlooking the river – what a wonderful sight!

It was from here that I first saw Halley's Comet. I find it impossible to describe the full beauty of this heavenly body which seemed to consist of a bright head suspended by a long luminous tail hanging from the sky. It was a sight I shall never forget.

While still at the rectory I became very interested in the church, having already known much of its history from my father. It was built by the Norman family of St Remy in 1170 and was known to be one of the most perfectly preserved Norman churches of its kind in the country. Famous for its Norman arches and elaborately carved doorways, the building consisted of chancel and nave with a massive embattled tower in the centre. I was particularly interested in the black marble font in which I was christened. It was nearly square with a round hollow, set in a short circular stone pedestal with four smaller ones at the angles. Three of these were of the twelfth century and one of the thirteenth. I vividly remember a doorway being discovered near to the pulpit showing a stairway leading up to the rood-loft. In those days the church was candle lit. These had always fascinated me, I had always wanted to know how many candles there were and how long it took to light them. It was not until I was staying at the rectory that the opportunity presented itself. One evening, when my uncle, who was parish clerk, arrived, it was to find me waiting outside the church door.

'Please, Uncle,' I murmured. 'Can I come in with you? I want to count the candles.'

He, being used to my peculiar requests, knew that I would not take no for an answer, so together we went into the darkened

S. MARY THE VIRGIN
IFFLEY   OXFORD

Iffley Church, the Church of S. Mary the Virgin, was built in the reign of Henry II (1154–89) by the Norman family of St Remy. They gave the land and his daughter Juliana's charter gave an 18d. yearly rent from Iffley Mill to the hospital of St John which later became Magdalen College. The patronage was given to Kenilworth Priory and by 1279 it had passed to the Archdeacon of Oxford, and it is now shared with the Dean and Chapter of Christ Church.

church. For the next fifteen minutes or so I was trying desperately hard to keep up with him and, at the same time, to count the candles.

Afterwards he said, 'Well, young lady, how many candles were there?'

'One hundred and twenty,' I answered.

As he never disputed it, I have always taken this to be the right number.

The churchyard, which adjoins the rectory on the north-west, I was able to explore by myself. For it was here my baby brother was buried near to the wall on the east side. A small tree that grew by the side of his grave, made me wonder whether it would grow to be as large as the yew tree on the south side of the churchyard, which is reputed to have been planted when the church was built. The new churchyard lies across the way near to the hillside. Here my parents, sister, and relatives are buried, and in 1982 a casket bearing the ashes of my elder brother was placed nearby.

Much of my early childhood was spent in or around the meadows which ran alongside the bottom of our lane. They were so lovely, especially in the spring, when after the flooding the water receded, and they became aglow with golden knobs (king cups) and white and mauve speckled snakeheads (fritillaries). On the swampy banks yellow iris grew in profusion. These were further enhanced by a pair of swans which returned each year to build their nest in the middle of one particular meadow. It was all so beautiful and made me realise how wonderful mother nature can be.

Their ever changing scenes still stand out in my memory. I remember on one occasion the river burst its banks. At the time I was playing in the lane and had scarcely time to reach the little bridge spanning the brook before the water meadows, lane and brook became as one huge expanse of water. As I watched the water getting higher and higher I was amazed to see large and small fish of every size and type being tossed into the brook like ninepins. They were literally tumbling over each other as they were swept helplessly away in a raging torrent of water. It was not until the water subsided that the full havoc of the floods could be seen. Hedges were torn down and on the banks of the brook lay the dead and mutilated bodies of the fish.

Then there was the haymaking season, when I used to help the men rake the grass into long rows to dry out in the hot sunshine. Afterwards I would watch them load it onto the wagon and then walk with them to the rickyard. On the return journey I was allowed to ride astride the old carthorse.

At midday there was a break for lunch, when the men made for the shade of the old willow trees. Their food, which was tied up in a red handkerchief, consisted of a large crust of bread and cheese washed down by a mug of ale poured from an old tin can. Then a clay pipe of tobacco and back to work.

During the hot summer months we would collect dried pieces of wood from the surrounding countryside, which my father would chop up and stock ready for making extra fuel for the winter.

I suppose the people I knew best were the Watson family, they lived in a detached house at the bottom of our lane. At that time Lily, the youngest of six was my constant companion. We spent many hours playing in and around the meadows, the hollow willow trees were made our home. They were quite easy to climb and seemed to have self made seats. Here we picnicked and pretended to entertain our friends. In the wintertime the meadows would freeze over and provide some good skating.

I remember one occasion seeing my friend take two chairs down to the meadow. On enquiring what she was doing, she said, 'You come and see.' I watched as she placed her chairs near the entrance to the meadow. A huge cardboard notice attached to the back of one chair denoted that it was for hire and could be used by skaters to change their shoes, etc. They also left any of their personal belongings in her care. When I saw this I thought what's sauce for the goose is sauce for the gander as the saying goes. So without more ado I rushed home and knowing my mother was out, I quickly removed two chairs from the room, carrying them down to the meadow and setting them up on the opposite side of the field. However, as our services became more and more in demand, so too, did our frozen limbs begin to take effect. Fortunately my friend solved the problem. Picking up her chairs and contents, she slowly advanced towards me and placing her chairs alongside mine, suggested we work together and share the proceeds. She also said we could take it in turns to pop across to her house, which was just across the lane, and have a warm. Being so cold I readily agreed. My friend won the toss to go first, leaving me to look after the customers. By the time she returned I could scarcely move my limbs. As I hobbled across the lane, her mother came to meet me and taking me into the house, gave me a nice hot cup of tea and sat me down in front of a roaring fire to thaw out, as she put it. Gradually my aching limbs began to thaw and by the time I returned to the meadow, my friend was beginning to pack up.

At the end of the afternoon we had collected one shilling and two pence, working out at seven pence each. To me this was a fortune, enough to buy two ounces of tea and some sugar. Picking up my chairs I hurried back to reach home before my mother arrived. How vividly I remember arranging my seven pennies across the table and then handing them to her, one at a time. Of course she wanted to know how I had come by them. After explaining, and also admitting that I had taken two of her chairs, she began to understand. I thought she would be overjoyed to receive so much money, instead I saw tears trickling down her cheeks. For a moment she was too overcome to speak. Then to my great surprise she handed the money back to me saying, 'The money is yours, take it to start your own savings account.' I needed no second bidding. Early the next morning I presented myself at the village sub-post office where I asked Miss Blay, the post mistress, for a savings card. I then handed over my seven pennies for seven penny stamps, which she affixed to my card. When eventually I had twelve stamps on my card, every penny I had earned from doing odd jobs, such as running errands, etc., I became the proud owner of a Post Office Savings Book. Take care of the pence and the pounds will take care of themselves, was a lesson that was to remain with me throughout my life.

Friday night was bath night. We took it in turns to be bathed. The zinc bath was placed in front of the fire. I was always the first and my hair was washed too then I was whisked out to dry my hair in front of the fire, and then to bed.

At the age of six I caught whooping cough and was not able to go to school. I remember my mother taking me with her to do shopping in order that I could pass by a road that was being tarred – this was supposed to do me good.

My sister, brother and I all had measles too! Fortunately my brother and I suffered no ill effects, but my sister, Alice, had it rather badly and for a time her eyesight was impaired. I remember for some time after, my mother had to put 'drops' in her eyes.

Our Cottage

From the outside our cottage was quite picturesque. Built of stone, its walls were covered in ivy and climbing roses. Nearest to the house was a flower garden and this was tended by my mother. The rest of the garden was given over to father for vegetables. In the centre of the garden was a marvellous Blenheim apple tree. It was always laden with fruit and when in blossom was admired by passers by.

When picking time came around, which was early October, my father would see that they were gathered with great care. It was my job to sort through the apples, picking out the small and bruised ones. The rest were then hand-picked ready to sell. We had our regular customers. They usually placed their orders well in advance. We sold them for two shillings and sixpence a bushel ($12\frac{1}{2}$p).

Alongside a wall ran a large chicken run. On either side of the house were farm buildings. At the back was a spinney and fields.

Facilities, such as wash-house, closet and water were shared with our next door neighbour. The water was pumped from a well in the corner of our garden. This meant that every time our neighbour wanted water, she had to pass by our door. This we did not mind, as the wash-house being the other side, the same thing applied. I remember the lavatory had a large hole in the centre of a very large white scrubbed box, with a smaller hole in the lower part for us children. About every six months it was my father's job to empty the earth closet, the contents of which he buried in a corner of the garden in a very deep hole. There was no lock on the lavatory door, but until my aunt, who had lived next door, moved to another part of the village, it never presented any problems.

When our new neighbour arrived, it was entirely different. She was a widow and undoubtedly a born snob. The idea of sharing the lavatory was to her most distasteful, and as for the wash-house, 'I always send my washing to the laundry,' she said.

My mother, who would never be drawn in to an argument, quietly reminded her that she didn't have to take the cottage, but having done so, she would be expected to help in keeping it clean.

2

Schooldays

IN THE OLDEN DAYS children could start school at the age of three, but this was not compulsory. My earliest recollection was when, at the age of four, my mother took me to school for the first time. It was more of a nursery class and was taken by what was then known as a pupil teacher. I remember we played with wooden bricks, plasticine, and looked at lovely picture books. At the age of five I moved over to the other side of the room, where the class was taken by another lady. Here we were given an insight on how to write and spell. After this I moved to the middle class room. A Miss Gaskin was my favourite teacher. She was middle aged and had a round plump face. Her lip was covered in moustache. She was a marvellous teacher and under her I quickly learned to read and write. My easy arithmetic greatly improved. She never used a cane, her form of punishment was to stay after school hours and write one hundred lines of what you had done wrong. This may seem crude, but it had the desired effect. Mrs Mason also taught me. She seemed a little old lady, slightly bent, with grey hair tightly drawn back and caught up in an old-fashioned bun on top of her head.

It is often said that teaching in those days was repetitive, but to me the standard of education was good. It comprised mostly of the three 'R's, which, in my opinion, is so sadly lacking in education today. My favourite subjects were Scripture, Recitation, History and Geography. I was quick to learn and delighted when I finally moved up into the 'top' class. Fortunately the headmaster, who I gathered often used the cane on children, had just retired, and a headmistress had been appointed.

Her name was Miss Kibblewhite. She was young and attractive

and for a time all the children were on their best behaviour. This, however, lulled her into a false sense of security. Some of the eleven-year-old boys were as tall as her and as their curiosity began to wear off, so they began to take advantage of her. At first she pretended to take little notice of their pranks, hoping no doubt that they would quickly tire of them. Unfortunately, she didn't know them and although they were in the minority, their influence on the other children was sufficient to bring the entire class into a state of uproar. She then tried the cane, but this was quite hopeless as each time the cane came down, the hand would be pulled away and would land with a terrific bang on the wooden desk, much to the amusement of the other children. As her indignation grew, she would drag the boy from his desk and with a great deal of struggling and kicking manage to shut him in the lobby until school was over. Girls were punished by having to stand in the classroom with their hands on their heads.

It being a mixed school I quickly learned to stick up for myself. I remember one girl in particular whose parents had recently come to live at Cowley. She was about ten years of age and had previously attended a private school. It did not take long for the other children to cotton on to this stranger. She was so different to the usual village children. She was shy and blushed easily and her clothes did not help, she wore a different dress for each day of the week. They were pretty, frilly dresses, much more suitable for a party than school wear. The boys took a great delight in throwing blobs of ink down the back of them. They then noticed that each dress was a different colour and began to nickname her according to the colour. I remember it was canary for yellow, greenfinch for green, beetrooty for red and so it went on, until the poor girl was reduced to tears.

In fact it became so bad that one of the teachers had to escort her home. This was finally reported to the vicar and school manager. They decided that she should no longer attend our school. The ringleaders were severely reprimanded for bringing disgrace on the school. These boys were in the minority and in fact, all belonged to the same family.

We always knew when the school inspector was due to arrive for his annual visit. Everything was tidied up and by the time he arrived all was 'spick and span'. No one could have been more nervous than the headmistress as she tried to encourage the children to be on their best behaviour. The register was inspected and a great deal of discussion took place with the teachers regarding absentees. Usually, there were perfectly genuine reasons such as children's ailments. In the case of playing truant, parents were visited and sometimes it was found they had no idea this was happening – then woe-betide the boy when he returned home, to receive a good strapping from his dad. In those days it was quite common for children to have fits. I remember one girl with lovely auburn hair. She would just swoon off with her eyes wide open. Another was a boy, who when his attacks were coming on would start to run, until finally he would fall to the ground, foaming at the mouth. When this happened it took several people to hold him down.

On the whole my school days were exceptionally happy. The annual prize giving was to me a great occasion, when it was with some pride that I began to receive prizes for various subjects. Books were always of great interest to me. Apart from the Bishop's prize, there were two I found most interesting. One was entitled *Golden Treasury* which contained all my favourite poems and the other was called *Wild Flowers and Their Wonderful Ways* written by the Revd Charles A. Hall. Apart from explaining all about wild flowers, it contained useful illustrations, both in colour and black and white. Other books I won were *Under One Standard, Spurs and Bride* by Gertrude Hollis and *The Starling*.

My greatest thrill was when I received a silver watch for five years never absent, never late. I gather this particular award was not resumed after World War One. The school and church lay at the far end of the village. The first school bell always rang at five to nine. I would try to leave home at 8.30 a.m. in order to arrive at school before the second bell went. I had to run all the way and would arrive breathless and near to tears.

As children we learned to be content with small mercies. We had no real pocket money. Occasionally one earned a halfpenny for running an errand for a neighbour and this was spent on sweets. I usually selected something that lasted a long time. A liquorice ribbon lasted and by the time it was finished, my face and tongue were as black as the liquorice. Another favourite was a sherbet dab.

One great occasion was when my teacher informed me that I had been chosen to sit for a scholarship to Milham Ford School. This was a comparatively new school, having been opened in Cowley Place, Oxford, in the year 1905. At that time only a few places were being made available for scholarships.

My friend, Marjorie Lines, who had attended Iffley School and had previously won a scholarship to this school, often discussed the school's curriculum with me which I gathered was of a very high standard. She also mentioned the upkeep involved and how expensive her mother found it in buying her school uniform, books etc. The latter was now my worry, as with my thoughts in a turmoil, I ran home to tell my mother.

I remember rushing into the house and blurting out, 'My teacher wants me to sit for a scholarship for Milham Ford School, but I know you can't afford it!' I told her that if I passed, she would have to pay for my school uniform and books.

'It was very different with Marjorie Lines,' I argued. 'Her mother does dressmaking, but you only have 15 shillings that dad gives you from his weekly pay packet.'

Looking back, I am sure my words must have hurt her for she replied, 'You know I would do anything for you, but what you say is right, I could not afford the upkeep.'

However, knowing how much this meant to me, she suggested I put the facts before my teacher and get her reaction.

This I did, and finally asked if my name could be withdrawn.

Oxfordshire Education Committee

Midsummer 1915.

IFFLEY School.

This **Certificate** is awarded to

Florence Kirby.

who, being entitled to a prize for

Good Conduct

and

Regular Attendance,

voluntarily and gladly relinquished it, desiring by this sacrifice to aid the Cause of Britain and Her Allies.

Attendances :

407 out of 407.

a. w. Hall

Chairman.

This Certificate of Good Conduct was presented to me shortly before I became a pupil teacher at Iffley school. Born in Iffley in 1901 my name was Agnes Florence Kirby, daughter of Richard William and Agnes Kirby formerly Cunnington.

Unfortunately she would not hear of it, remarking, 'Sit for it first and we will talk it over afterwards.'

This in no way allayed my fears and for the first time in my life, I realised what it really meant to be poor. So when the day came, it was with mixed feelings that I presented myself at the school. Here I met girls from other schools, most of them laughing and joking together. I wondered if they were really feeling as nervous as I was?

However, we were not left long to our own devices before a teacher arrived. She escorted us to a large classroom where the exam took place. I had received no previous preparation and when I saw the type of sums we were expected to do, I realised how unprepared I was. It was all advanced arithmetic, which at that time I had not even been taught. However, I did my best and hoped that my other subjects would make up for it.

After lunch we were told that the headmistress would be interviewing us separately and also would be taking recitation. I remember how proud I felt when being ushered into her room and introduced as Florence Kirby from Iffley School.

She was a very charming person and quickly put me at ease as with a nod and a smile she asked me to sit down. Then, after a few questions, I was asked to recite something of my own choice and I recited the first four verses and the last verse of Elegy, written in a Country Churchyard, by Thomas Gray.

At the end she remarked, 'Excellent, you have a wonderful memory and a nice speaking voice.'

This really made my day and I went home feeling very happy. When I attended school the next day, my teacher wanted to know all about the examination papers, and if I thought I had done well. However, all we could do was to wait until the result came through. The waiting seemed endless. Had I passed, I wondered? Then one morning the Head called me to her desk and there outspread lay the result. Reading, writing, recitation and verbal questions were considered good, but apparently not good enough for a pass.

As I grew older I tended to keep to girls more of my own age. Often, after school hours we would play games together. On one occasion we were playing a game called hopscotch and had just finished marking out the squares when, to our astonishment, we saw four gentlemen approaching. They were walking two abreast, they all wore bowler hats and were wearing smart suits. This, to us, was most unusual and we stopped our game to watch their approach. As they drew nearer I whispered excitedly to my playmates, 'It's the Prince of Wales!'

At this they burst out laughing and told me not to be so silly. However, not to be outdone, I waited until they had passed and then, to their astonishment, I called out, 'Hello, Your Royal Highness.'

At this the two in front hesitated and then momentarily stopped. I was scared stiff they were going to report me to the police, but to my great surprise he turned, smiling, and waved a small cane he was carrying. Then to my great relief they walked onwards to the church. My friends still did not believe it was the Prince, until the following day an article appeared in the local press. This stated that the Prince of Wales had visited Iffley Church, afterwards returning by way of the tow-path, where at the toll gate he was asked for his halfpenny.

My aunt, who was a cripple, used to take the money at the toll gate and when I said, 'Fancy asking the Prince for his halfpenny!' She replied, 'That is the charge. Had it been the King of England himself, he would still have been asked to pay the toll fee.'

Hide and seek was another favourite game. This was a mixed game often played with boys and girls. We had great fun in and out of the copse, pitting our skills against the boys. Sometimes we hid in the long grass, but this was not so good as, having left our trail, we were easily found, often with dire results. The boys would carry small frogs in their hands and when catching up with us, would put them down the back of our necks. There were then shrieks of terror from the girls and loud laughter from the boys as they watched us shaking ourselves until the frogs finally fell out.

My recollection of May Day was the one in which I actually took part. Having been chosen as May Queen, it was later discovered the only boy suitable for King, was so much shorter than myself so it became necessary to elect a new Queen. I remember my disappointment as the following year I would have been too old to take part. I was allowed to go as one of the maids of honour. The retinue was made up of about thirty children between the ages of nine and eleven.

It was an exciting time. The preparations seemed endless. For weeks beforehand we practised the traditional May songs until the teacher was satisfied that we knew them by heart. Then there was the route and order of procession to be mapped out well in advance.

Next came the flowers for decorating our hats and maypoles. Apart from the May Queen who carried a sheaf of arum lilies given by Mrs Allen of Wootten House, each one of us was responsible for providing our own flowers and evergreens. Usually these could be found in our own gardens, but where this was not possible, neighbours and friends came to our rescue. Any surplus flowers or greenery was taken back to the school and used to decorate the garlands and collecting box.

It was a pretty sight as on May Morning we all assembled at the school to be inspected by the headmistress. The Queen looked splendid carrying her lovely sheaf of lilies held together with white ribbon and tied in a large bow. We girls all wore white frocks with wreaths of flowers on our heads. The boys, dressed in their Sunday best, carried coloured wooden poles dressed in flowers and evergreens and topped with a crown imperial.

The procession, headed by the King and Queen, maids of honour, garlanders, treasurers, guards, mace bearers and two older boys acting as policemen, moved off to attend a short service in the church.

Our first point of call was at the vicarage, where in the garden under the mulberry tree, we sang our May songs. Our approach through the village was heralded by the singing of:

Hark, the birds begin their lay,
Flow'rets deck the robe of May;
See the little lambkins bound,
Playful o'er the clover ground.
Where the yellow cowslips grow,
There the sportive heifers low,
And around us everywhere
Insect tribes disport the air.

Every heart with joy shall glow,
Rural pleasures banish woe,
Bells shall ring and all be gay,
This is nature's holiday.

Now the nymphs and swains advance
O'er the lawn in cheerful dance,
Garlands from the hawthorn bow
Grace the happy shepherd's brow;
While the maidens in array
Crown the happy Queen of May;
Innocence, content and love,
Fill the meadow and the grove.

Every heart with joy shall glow,
Rural pleasures banish woe,
Bells shall ring and all be gay,
This is nature's holiday.

Here and there we would pause to make a collection from people who had gathered at their doorways to watch us pass by. At some of the big houses the King was asked to kiss the Queen. After a great deal of teasing and hesitation, this was finally accomplished. We were then rewarded with an extra sixpence in our money box.

After calling at all the large houses in the village, we then wended our way down the Iffley Road. Our last point of call was a home for elderly ladies in Stanley Road. Here we sang by the bedside of some of the residents. They were delighted to see us and, apart from helping to fill our money box, they rewarded us with re-freshment and sweets.

After this we returned to the village and after a short rest at home, we were ready to join the other schoolchildren for tea. The tea was paid for from money collected. Any surplus money was divided among those having taken part. I remember we each received one shilling and three pence and the King and Queen received two shillings.

During the school holidays there was a time when most of my friends left the village to stay with relatives in the surrounding districts, such as Thame or Abingdon, which although only a few miles away, to me, in those days, seemed miles away. How I envied them especially my sister, Alice, who always spent her school holidays with an uncle and aunt at a small village in Gloucestershire.

Nevertheless I was never lonely. I loved the river and each day I would go swimming at the Long Bridges bathing place. In the evening I could hire a punt for sixpence (2½p) and providing I promised to tie it up safely when I returned, I was allowed to have it as long as I liked. Another pastime was helping a lady pick her fruit. Her name was Mrs Walters and she lived at Donnington Cottage. She was very deaf, but we had an arrangement permitting me to look over her house, and if not in, she would be down the garden. It was a rambling old garden. If she was behind some of the bushes I would take quite a time to find her, and she being so deaf it was no use my calling out.

To converse with her was quite impossible, but as I knew her so well, I found little difficulty in understanding what she wanted me to do. After picking the fruit we would return to the house for a nice tea, which was my reward for helping. Then there was an old lady that I used to visit, usually on my way home from school. She lived in a small cottage at the far end of Baker's Lane. She was known to everyone in the village as Granny Reeves, a name no doubt derived from the fact she had brought up nineteen children, including foster children. When I knew her she lived with her daughter, Kitty, and an adopted son named Charles.

I remember her as a little old lady sitting in a comfortable armchair, her grey hair peeping from beneath a white laced bonnet, and her shoulders covered with a brightly coloured knitted shawl. Although well over ninety, she still retained a great sense of humour. Sitting by her side, she would take my hand and with an occasional pat on my shoulder, would ask about my school lessons and whether I had been a good girl. When we had a new headmistress she was very interested, and wanted to know all about her. Was she young or old, married or single? She was highly amused on being told she was single, but there was a young man who called for her each day after school lessons.

She always liked to hear about the local gossip. 'Had Mrs Saxon's baby been born yet?' or 'What was the new vicar like?' After a while she would fumble beneath her apron and produce a bag of sweets. When this happened I knew she was tired and wanted me to go. So I would take one sweet and hand them back to her knowing when next I called, the same bag of sweets would be produced. When she died the whole village mourned her passing. I remember seeing her in her coffin. She looked so sweet and serene that I could not help thinking how peaceful death was.

After the funeral I walked slowly through the village pausing only a few moments to gaze up Baker's Lane where only a short while before Granny Reeves had gone on her last journey. I had indeed lost a friend.

During the year the vicar visited most cottages. When he knocked on the doors, there was always a great deal of shuffling within. As we had a long garden path leading to our cottage, we were able to see who was approaching in good time. 'Here's the vicar', mother would say and by the time he had knocked on the door, the whole room would be made to look spic and span. Mother's apron was quickly removed and she would receive him with a curtsy. After placing a chair for him, she would suggest a cup of tea, together with a piece of home-made cake. He never refused, Mother afterwards remarking, 'I doubt very much whether he had any lunch, let alone tea!' He would rise from his seat, assuring Mother he was much refreshed and ready to visit a few more parishioners.

When he first came to the parish, his daughter, Audrey, attended the village school. At that time she was a real tomboy and delighted joining games and pranks with the other children. Unfortunately I don't think her parents approved, for she was shortly removed and taught by a governess. She was a nice girl and my mother told me she loved to spend most of her spare time in the kitchen. One Christmas she gave me a double-jointed doll. It had a most adorable round rosy face, opened and closed its eyes, had fair hair and lovely eyelashes. It had clothes that I could take off and put on, a blue dress and its underclothes were white and lace trimmed. Its little socks and shoes also came off. She was my baby! I neatly folded her clothes and put them into the box each night.

Once a week on a Friday, mother would walk into Oxford and do her main shopping in Cowley Road. In Cowley Road were the grocers, Home and Colonial, Maypole and Butlers. During the week we bought other things at the village shop. A cottage loaf cost 3*d.* and was delivered by a baker from the village. This was our favourite. Father used to take the detachable top and a lump of cheese for his midday meal. Milk was delivered to the door and cost 2*d.* a pint. Skimmed milk, used for puddings, was 1*d.* a quart. ¼lb of tea cost 4½*d* and we usually bought 2 ozs. Lamp oil (paraffin) 2*d.*, sugar 2*d.* lb, eggs 18 for one shilling, whisky three shillings a bottle. Coal varied between 15*s.* and £1 for a ton, Red Bell tobacco 2½*d.* an oz. Wages were 18*s.* per week and the old age pension 5*s.* a week. Bread and jam was our usual meal at teatime, butter at one shilling a pound was too expensive. Allotments were a premium in those days, all beautifully kept. Many reserved a small plot for flowers and usually a strawberry bed. Potatoes, peas and broad beans were among some of the finest vegetables grown. Our neighbours, who lived in the house at the bottom of the lane, always kept their own pigs. They, at least, were assured of plenty of food. We only kept hens, we were always sure of a good supply of eggs and an occasional chicken for Sunday dinner. The cock could be heard crowing from early dawn. My mother made rhubarb and elderberry wine.

Pedlars and hawkers brought their wares for sale on anything available that could be pushed around. Some had old prams, whilst other brought their goods by donkey and cart. Then there was the knife grinder, he usually did a good trade grinding scissors.

There were no restrictions on keeping pigs and pig killing was common. Three or four men would arrive and in no time at all we would hear the pig squealing.

It seemed to me that everything from the pig was used for food. Even the blood was caught in a bucket and used for making hog's pudding. The pig's head was boiled and made into brawn and the pig's feet were boiled to a mass of jelly. The nicer parts – bacon and ham – used to make my mouth water. At Christmas, we would visit the market. Pigs hung upside down with an orange in their mouths, and in all the stalls holly and mistletoe hung with fruit and nuts for the festive season. The shops were grand with lovely dolls displayed in boxes, beautiful picture books and an unbelievable array of toys.

Of course, I knew I was only being taken to see them in the shops. I knew we could not afford to buy any, but it was lovely seeing them.

Then there were errands to be run. Certain people would stand at their gates waiting for the children to come out of school and then call on them to run an errand. In this way we earned an odd penny or two.

Father belonged to a slate club run by the pub, which helped in the case of illness. He paid a shilling a month and if sick received a small weekly benefit. At Christmas there was a share out of the unused balance. I remember my father saying, 'There won't be much of a share out this year, there's been too many pay-outs for illness.' It helped to buy a few extras for Christmas.

Money from the thrift club was used to buy clothes. A suit could be bought for just over a pound, socks and shirts for the men and an occasional dress or two-piece (coat and dress) for the girls. Then of course boots. Usually we took it in turns to have something new. How my mother managed, I'll never know. After my brother came home from the First World War, he used to make my father a suit, but as his eyesight was so badly impaired, he later had to give this up.

There was a sort of fund to which my mother contributed in case medical attention was needed. Fortunately we had no serious illnesses. For the few ailments that arose, mother had her own remedies. These included Beecham's Pills for constipation, hot beer and ginger for a cold, nettle tea imbibed in the spring to cool down the blood, camphorated oil on cotton wool for ear ache and liniment for back and neck pains.

I have vivid recollections of my early childhood. Born to a poor, but much respected family I was the youngest of four children, a sister and two brothers. I never knew my brother Richard, he died in infancy. Reg was the eldest, then came Alice and myself.

We lived in a small semi-detached stone built cottage, two up and two down. The back bedroom formed part of the landing. Downstairs was a pantry and living room. Both rooms had stone slab floors. These were covered with highly polished oilcloth and brightly coloured home-made rugs. The living room consisted of two tables, one plain white wood. This was used for meals and when not in use was covered by a pretty designed tapestry cloth. The other was a dark oak pedestal table. On this rested the family bible and various photographs. Four wooden and two cane-seated chairs, together with two armchairs and a sofa, completed the furniture.

In the centre of the room was a high mantelpiece, underneath this a small fireplace, with hobs either side. When cooking, I remember my mother would place two narrow iron bars across, and in this way she was able to keep all saucepans boiling together, plus the kettle for a cup of tea. The oven was heated by a continued process of poking red-hot embers of coal underneath. On one side of the fireplace was a large cupboard, which formed part of a dresser. On this stood a beautifully polished brass lamp. On the shelves above was a lovely family china tea-service. The front door opened directly into the living room. In the wintertime it was extremely cold and although a thick curtain hung behind the door, it was impossible to exclude the draught. We children slept in the back bedroom in two single iron bedsteads, my sister and I sleeping one either end, the other was used by my brother. Before getting into bed, we were taught to kneel and say our prayers. These consisted of the Lord's prayer and God Bless Mummy and Daddy. Being afraid of the dark, I was always allowed to have a small brass tumbling lamp, so named, that if it was knocked over, it would right itself. Even so, for added safety it was placed on a high bracket out of my reach. The rent of the cottage at that time was two shillings and sixpence a week (12½p).

3

Parents and Relatives

MY FATHER came from Middle Barton, a small village in Oxfordshire. His father was a tailor and also kept the general store. I never met him, but I do remember meeting his mother once on Oxford Station.

My father was a very independent person. I gathered from my mother he had had a very strict upbringing. He was the eldest of five, and after leaving school he refused to take part in the family business and left home at a very early age to try his fortune in the outside world. I understand it was not too successful as he later returned to the family fold and met my mother.

He was of medium height and well built. He had a round pleasant face with twinkling blue eyes, curly black hair, and a small moustache which he always kept well trimmed. He worked at the local brewery in Oxford and left home every morning at about 5.30 a.m. to walk the three miles. On his way home he would sometimes call in at one of the local pubs in the area. Here he would meet some of his pals, when it would develop into a drinking orgy. Although he never touched spirits, the amount of beer drank on an empty stomach, was sufficient to take effect.

On these occasions, which were rare, I would sit up to keep my mother company until he returned. We could always hear him coming up the garden path and this gave me time to get to bed before he reached the door. My mother never remonstrated with father whilst in drink, but would always try to humour him and coax him into eating his supper. When this was not possible, she would help him gently up the stairs to bed, afterwards coming into my bedroom to kiss me goodnight and assure me all was well.

My father was normally quite charming and often amusing.

Although he had many faults, he was at heart a deeply religious man. He had a great love of music and for many years sang in the church choir.

I never heard him swear. I well remember my brother, when returning from one of his summer camps with the Territorials, let slip a swear word. He was quickly brought to heel by my father who remarked, 'Don't ever let me hear that language in this house again.'

Although he resented his own upbringing he was never backward in applying it to his own family. I remember on one occasion it was decided that my father and I should visit some of his relatives at Middle Barton. I wore a pretty pale blue dress with little flounces and father was wearing his best Sunday suit and bowler hat. We were already waiting at the top of the lane at 7 a.m. when the carrier's cart came along to pick us up.

To me this was wonderful. As we rattled along, I thought now I shall have something to tell the other children and write about when I return to school.

We were dropped at a place called Hopcroft's Holt and from there we had to walk the remaining distance. It was a long walk, up hill and down dale. At last we reached the village. Our first point of call was at the house of Uncle Felix. He kept the village shop. Father rang the bell and we both waited nervously on the doorstep. The door was opened by a middle-aged woman who I took to be my aunt. You can imagine my embarrassment as we waited on the doorstep and heard her announce, 'Mr Kirby and daughter have arrived, Ma'am.'

Even Father had forgotten what his sister looked like. Uncle Felix was sitting in his chair, but as we approached he rose to greet us, me with a gentle pat on my head, and a hearty hand shake with Father.

Then Aunt Marian suggested I wash my hands and I was led away, first to the loo and then to my cousin's bedroom to tidy up. When I returned father was in deep conversation with my uncle.

Dinner was then served in the dining room by the maid. She brought it in and as uncle carved the joint, she handed it round. We helped ourselves to vegetables. Aunt Marian served the sweet, which I remember was apple tart with cream. There was an orchard consisting of many fruit trees. Beyond this was a large field where grazed a horse and cows lay chewing the cud.

I had met my two cousins, Winnie and Mona. They were nice girls and later both became schoolteachers.

My mother was so different from father. She was the peacemaker. In her youth she must have been quite beautiful. She was short, with lovely dark hair which was drawn back from the forehead and twisted into a bun at the back. She spoke little of her early life. I understand she met my father when in service at Middle Barton. At that time she was walking out with his brother, Felix. He, I gathered, was an entirely different person to my father and much thought of by his parents.

But on the prodigal son's return, he apparently appealed more, for better or worse, to my mother, and much against the wishes of his parents and her own, she married him. In later life when things went wrong, I often heard her say, 'I should have listened to his parents.'

She was the eldest of four, three sisters and one brother. She came from an old Iffley family who had lived in the village for generations. Her father had been a master stonemason, as was his father before him. I recall seeing her father's signature in the family bible, written in beautiful copperplate writing. I cannot help thinking it would put to shame many of the illegible signatures we see today. One could almost picture the pen and ink and the pride he took in entering his and his children's names, legible for all times.

How I wish the bible had come to me after my father's death. But, alas, it went to my brother. When, after his death, I saw it, the pages relating to the family tree were missing.

On Sundays my father wore a choker collar and a starched white detachable front called a dicky. Because of the stiffness, he found

My mother, when young. She was born on the 21st January 1858 in Iffley. Her name was Agnes Cunnington, daughter of John and Lucy Cunnington formerly Hurst, and her father was a stonemason.

great difficulty in fastening it and mother was often called to the rescue.

My mother's sister, Aunt Bessie, was in service at Petersfield in Hampshire, where she worked as a cook-housekeeper. She always came to stay with us for her annual holiday. How we dreaded her coming. Even my mother seemed scared of her. Father kept out of her way as much as possible. We all had to be on our best behaviour.

She was a well-preserved woman, nicely dressed and well spoken. Her silver grey hair was covered with a fine hair net. I remember she wore a veil and on arrival this would be raised just long enough to implant a kiss on our cheeks. Then, before going upstairs to unpack, she would settle herself in her favourite chair and wait for mother to bring her a cup of tea.

Indoors, she always wore a fur cape around her shoulders – how I longed to caress it, but I knew this was forbidden. She brought her own food for my mother to cook. For tea she would have huge hunks of new bread thickly spread with real butter. We kids

My parents outside our cottage.

used to watch open-mouthed, until finally mother would be called to send us into the garden until she had finished her tea.

I used to call her 'stuck up, greedy guts' and I got the impression that as she did not approve of my mother's marriage, she took this way of showing it.

I vividly remember some years later she was taken ill and entered hospital. Whilst there, she spoke to my mother of her savings in the Post Office Savings Bank, and how in the case of anything happening to her, she wished it to come to her. When mother heard of this she tried to persuade her to draw some of it out and spend it on a few luxuries during her lifetime, but she would not hear of it.

When she died and mother went to the Post Office to withdraw the money, they wanted to know where she had died. On hearing in hospital, they said they would have to first contact the hospital to find out if anything was owing. As was the case in those days, the hospital claimed the lot. I remember mother even had to pay the funeral expenses. Such was her nature that not once did she show the slightest rancour towards her sister, who during her lifetime had owed her so much.

My mother's brother, Philip, lived in a nice detached house in Mill Lane, Iffley. He was the Parish Clerk and the village undertaker. I remember the beautiful garden that led down to the river and the Old Mill. It had a wonderful variety of fruit trees, including greengage, victoria plum, damson and apple. There were raspberries and strawberries, also gooseberry and currant bushes. On the wall in front of the house was a marvellous grapevine. The bunches hung in huge clusters and when they were turning colour, it was quite a sight.

Also in the garden was a large wooden workshop. It was raised some distance from the ground with small wooden steps which led to the entrance. It was here that I used to watch my uncle making coffins. It was a revelation to me to watch him at work. I would watch wide eyed as bit by bit the coffin would be completed. On me asking, 'How do you know it will fit the person?' he explained this was done by measurements.

To me, this was all very sad, especially if the person had been known to me all my life. It meant losing a friend. I remember on one occasion he was making a small white coffin for a little child who had died in the village. Being curious, I asked my uncle why it was white to which he replied that it denoted purity.

'Does that mean she will go to heaven?' I asked

He looked up, smiled, and replied, 'You ask too many questions, young lady.'

He had six children, Gladys was the youngest. She married Jim Barton, who lived at the Isis Hotel on the river. Violet, the eldest, lived at home and helped her mother with the housework.

Iffley Mill, Oxford, prior to being burnt down in 1908.

They were a happy family, so much so, that when two of his own children died he was so upset he decided he could no longer continue as undertaker.

Mother's other sister lived in the adjoining cottage. Although slightly crippled from birth, it in no way prevented her from getting around.

I remember after Iffley Mill was burnt down, a small wooden hut was erected and it was from here that she collected the halfpennies at the toll gate. During the summer months many people passed this way to Iffley lock and the riverside walk. Some people would try to pass without paying, but were quickly brought to heel by my Aunt's firm request for 'your halfpenny please.'

A bye-law forbade any 'body' being carried through the toll gate. When a person died, the body was punted across the river to the opposite bank.

4

After School

WORLD WAR I broke out while I was still at school. This made a tremendous difference to my life.

At first I thought it was great fun, but when my brother, who was already in the Territorial Army, was called up, everything changed.

When I left school I wanted to do office work or be a telephonist at the GPO. In fact I did apply for the latter and received a letter asking me to go for a voice test, but unfortunately when I showed the letter to my mother, my hopes were dashed to the ground.

For the time being I was allowed to take on a temporary job at Taunt's Printing Works on Cowley Road, Oxford. I worked with another girl setting up type by hand. I found the work tedious, but very interesting.

I vividly remember seeing two men enter the works one morning. One was nicely dressed, whilst the other wore clothes which looked very shabby. He had a long flowing beard which seemed to cover the entire lower part of his face. This, together with very bushy eyebrows, was to me a little frightening.

I thought they were just visiting the works, until suddenly they stopped just opposite to where I was working. Then, pointing across, the shabby one approached me remarking 'You're a new girl!'

He wanted to know my name and what work I was doing. Where did I live? When I replied 'Iffley', he said, 'You're lucky, you have a beautiful church there and the lovely River Thames running nearby.' He was particularly interested to know that I loved the river and that for sixpence any evening I could hire a punt from the boathouse near to the free Ferry providing I tied it up safely on my return.

He laughed when I said, 'Of course, there are no cushions, only the bare struts, but as I love the river, I am quite happy just punting.'

He replied, 'That's my girl.'

Then with a pat on my shoulder, he left. I had no idea who he was.

I asked the girl I worked with, who, to my surprise replied, 'He's the gaffer, he lives here at the house called Riviera.' I was sorry that during the short time I worked there, I never saw him again.

In any case my mother had just heard of a lady living in the village who required a young girl to train as a house-parlour maid. I applied and got the job. I was informed my wages would be £12 a year paid monthly. I would be allowed one afternoon off each week, plus an evening off every alternate Sunday. My parents considered this good, especially as it would mean one less mouth to feed. During the interview I was given a list of clothes I would be expected to wear. For mornings, a striped cotton dress and white apron, in the afternoons, a black dress with stiff white cuffs, a frilly white apron and laced cap.

My mother bought all these ready made from Capes in St Ebbes, Oxford. This to me seemed a very expensive outlay and one that I promised to pay back. How well I remember packing my few personal belongings into a small tin trunk, at the same time listening to the reassuring voice of my mother that all would be well. The trunk was duly collected by carrier and taken to the house the night before I arrived.

Denton House, being only about ten minutes walk from my home meant I was able to keep back my morning wear, so that in the morning I was ready for work when I arrived. I had strict instructions from my mother to be sure to approach the house by the second drive, marked tradesmen's entrance. On arrival at the back door I timidly rang the bell. The door was opened by a middle-aged person who turned out to be Gertrude, the cook. She introduced me to Annie, the parlour maid, who I gathered I should be working under. After lunch, Annie and Gertrude showed me to the bedroom that I was to share with them. It was a large room in the attic. There were three beds, well spaced out, together with separate washing facilities.

Whilst I was changing in to my afternoon attire, they told me a little about the household. The mistress, Mrs Lever, was a kindly person and well liked by the staff. Her husband was a retired army major, very deaf, and inclined to be rude to the staff. Try not to displease him, they warned. They had one son. He was a captain in the regular army. When on leave he and his wife came to stay with his parents. Having by this time finished dressing I left them until teatime whilst I returned to duties downstairs. This being a quiet period, I took time to explore as much of the house as possible. Apart from the attic, I discovered there were four bedrooms and two gentleman's dressing rooms, all approached by a long corridor. Downstairs was a large dining room, a lounge, together with three other rooms, apparently mostly used when entertaining guests.

The servants' quarters consisted of a very large cheerless looking kitchen, a scullery and a small sitting room. Along a passage hung a row of bells, over which a large notice hung, denoting the number of each room.

Outside was a large garden. This was tended by an elderly gardener by the name of Treadaway. He was also responsible for filling up the coal scuttles.

My first encounter with the major was at dinner. I was handing round the vegetables, when he suddenly looked up to enquire my name.

When I replied 'Florence,' he bellowed, 'What is your other name?'

'Agnes,' I replied.

He said, 'Then that is the name you will be known by.'

I hated the name. However, when I returned to the kitchen Annie informed me that the mistress's name was also Florence, and with the major being deaf, he was always shouting for Florence to help. Naturally this could have been very embarrassing.

During my training I seemed to be 'Jack of all trades'. Rising at 6 a.m., it was my job to clean and light the fires in the dining room and study, clean the carpets and dust all rooms, then to polish the brass on the front door and wash over and polish the tiles in the hall, also clean all the shoes.

There being no bathroom meant I had to fill cans of hot water from the kitchen, carry them upstairs and place them outside the bedroom doors. The major had a hip bath and this was placed in his dressing room together with a large can of hot water for topping up. Then I knocked on his bedroom door and waited until he emerged. Otherwise he would declare the water was cold. When this happened he would ring for his bath to be emptied and renewed again with hot water. This occurred on two occasions and although his wife told him it was his fault for not coming sooner, he continued to blame Agnes.

After a quick breakfast, I then had to be ready at 9 a.m. to help serve breakfast in the dining room. After this I was upstairs with Annie to help make the beds and clean and dust the rooms, then be ready to clear away the breakfast when the bell rang.

After this I returned to my normal duties in the pantry, this being a small room mostly used for cleaning the silver and knives. I remember we had a knife cleaner. Annie showed me how to use it. By placing a knife in a small aperture and turning the handle, this caused the brushes to revolve. However, it was not until I had buckled two knives that Annie told me I had placed the blades the wrong way round.

At home my mother had a knife board on which she used a damp cork dipped in knife powder. This she rubbed on and after a wash in hot water they were left bright and clean. When we had fish the smell was removed by pushing the knife blade up and down in the garden soil, and then thoroughly washing it. After the knife episode things quietened down and I was beginning to like the job. Then one morning the major's bell rang in his dressing room and continued ringing until I reached the door. On entering I was horrified to find every book had been taken from the bookcase to show I had left a speck of dust on one shelf.

He literally bellowed his commands, at the same time banging on the floor with a heavy stick he used for walking. I was really terrified until his wife came along to find out what was happening. Then it fell to her to make the peace. 'Alright dear,' she said, 'Agnes understands and will do it after you leave your dressing room.'

After this I could stand no more. Fortunately, it being my afternoon off, I was able to tell my mother about it and that I would be giving in my notice to leave. She, seeing my distress, quite agreed. So I duly gave in my notice saying, 'I want to do my bit for my King and Country.' My mistress thought I was quite mad. However, this was my first and last job of so-called service. Slavery would have been a better name.

There was no doubt that the Great War solved many problems, including unemployment, for when it started in 1914 there was a rush to join the forces. My father, who had been out of work on and off since the strikes, tried three times to enlist, each time being refused on account of age limit. However, by the end of 1915 people of all ages were being accepted, and he joined the Army Veterinary Corps. This, I thought would be good news to my mother, who would now at least be receiving an Army Allowance. Therefore, when I finally left service, I was very surprised to hear that so far no money had been received. This being so, I advised her to write to his Commanding Officer. This she did and his reply somewhat astounded her. This was to say that my father had reported he was in such a hurry to join up, he forgot to state he was married!

Mother said afterwards, 'That is the kind of thing your dad would do.'

A marriage certificate was requested before any payment could be made. Judging from a letter received from my father, he was not too pleased, apparently he had received a severe reprimand from his Commanding Officer. I shall never forget this ordeal which nearly resulted in my mother taking her life.

Miss Armstrong, who lived in the village, had been appointed to help families until their allowance came through and she eventually advanced my mother some money which she repaid on a weekly basis.

My brother was already in the Territorials, and was actually in Camp when war was declared. By the time he returned home, his call-up papers were awaiting him. He immediately joined the Oxford and Bucks Light Infantry and was quickly drafted to France.

My sister, who had already enlisted, was stationed on Salisbury Plain. So when I finally left service it was not surprising that I, too, wanted to serve my King and Country. When my mother heard of this she suggested I was too young and inexperienced.

However, a few weeks later a notice appeared in the local press. This asked for recruits to serve as waitresses in a newly opened Officers' Mess. She then finally gave her consent.

So, being only fifteen at the time, and having no experience of military life, I ventured to apply. On arriving at the recruiting office I knocked on the opened door and nervously walked in. There I was met with a hive of activity, all appeared far too busy to even notice, let along attend to me. On looking round I noticed a man in uniform seated at a large desk.

Slowly I went across saying, 'I would like to join the Royal Flying Corps.'

He, without looking up, put out his hand saying, 'Medical.' I wondered what he was talking about until he said, 'I shall want a medical certificate from your doctor.'

So off I went to my doctor, who without any examination, made out a medical certificate.

Having run the two miles there and back, I arrived at the recruiting office somewhat breathless. Fortunately, this time I was met by a young woman in uniform. She asked me my name and address, then gave me a form to sign. I was then told to be at Carfax at 6.20 a.m. on the following Friday, where a tender would be waiting to transport me and eleven more recruits to our destination.

Apart from telling me I should be billeted at home and that my wage would be twelve shillings weekly, no mention of uniform was discussed.

On the Friday morning I cycled to Carfax where I was joined by the other recruits. The driver, having slung my bicycle on the back of the tender, then transported us to the Officers' Mess, which we found had been newly erected on farmland at Wolvercote. Here we were met by an orderly, who having shown us round, suggested we elect a Leader. As all of us except one were under twenty years of age, we suggested the eldest should be appointed.

Her name was Rhoda, aged about 25. Fortunately she accepted. We then left her to find out the procedure and working of the Mess. She reported the orderly had been quite helpful. He, himself, was quite pleased to hear we were all local girls and therefore quite conversant with the layout of the Mess in relation to the airfield. He was therefore quite happy to leave this side of the business to Rhoda.

So without any uniform or regimental discipline, our leader took over, and by the time some of the air crews arrived, everything was in order. The men seemed very surprised to be waited on by young girls, all wearing their pretty dresses, and judging by their remarks, this was more to their liking. We were a happy crowd and soon got in to the routine business of the day.

But not for long, as one morning in walked a woman in smartly dressed officer's uniform. For a moment silence reigned as she eyed us up and down. Then in true regimental voice she shouted, 'What is this, no uniform, no discipline, why was I not informed by headquarters? Who is in charge?'

We quickly presented our self appointed leader who nervously

In 1916 I joined the Royal Flying Corps. Originally no uniform was provided, but this was eventually rectified. However, when the airfield on Port Meadow, Oxford, was closed down, I was demobilised.

approached the officer, as together they moved off to the lower part of the Mess.

On their return we were all lined up. Our measurements were taken and we were informed that our uniforms would be issued in a few days. They arrived, and with them came Miss Battleaxe as we called her.

After inspection we were told to be ready at 9.30 a.m. the next morning when she would be taking us on a route march. As instructed all twelve of us were ready and waiting when she arrived. After lining us up in twos, we were given our marching orders, and off we went. First past the Sergeants' Mess, to be greeted by whistles and catcalls, then on through the village of Wolvercote as far as Port Meadow. Here we rested before returning to the Mess to prepare for lunch. After this we were once again left to our usual routine.

Eventually Miss Battleaxe reappeared, this time to inform us that the airfield on Port Meadow was closing down. We could either work in the Sergeants' Mess, join the Women's Army Auxiliary corps and see service overseas, or be demobilised.

We all chose to be demobbed.

So ended my career in the Royal Flying Corps. It was shortly after this that the name was changed to the Royal Air Force as we know it today.

5

Love Affairs

THE NEXT FEW WEEKS were spent looking for a job. Of one thing I was certain, never again would I return to domestic service. My work during the war had given me an entirely different outlook on life. I had grown up.

With my brother being married and my sister living away from home, mother was glad of my company. This being so, I made up my mind I would take time to decide what I wanted to do. In the mornings I helped my mother with the shopping and housework.

My afternoons being free, I would wander down the lane across the meadow, until I came to the riverbank. Here, under the willow trees, I would stretch out on the grass and read to my heart's content. It was all so beautiful and peaceful, but for an occasional boat or steamer passing by, I had the world to myself.

It was on one such afternoon, as I was watching a fish somersault in and out of the water, that I suddenly became aware of someone watching me. As I glanced up I noticed a man in uniform passing by in a canoe. Momentarily our eyes met, then he was gone. Shortly afterwards he returned, and drawing into the bank, commented on the weather and the beautiful surroundings. He was going further down the river.

'Would you join me?' he asked. This seemed to me an ideal way to enjoy a lovely afternoon, and so I gladly accepted.

He was of medium height, not particularly handsome, and he had fair hair and blue eyes. I soon learned his name was Morgan Roberts, that he had been stationed at Keble College, but was now staying at the Randolph Hotel. With the war being over he would shortly be returning to the States. He told me he came

Morgan Roberts at home in his study. In his bookcase he had placed my book of poems entitled The Golden Treasury.

from Superior, Wisconsin. He had two sisters and one brother, one sister was married and lived in Michigan. I told him about myself and my family. He was deeply interested in Iffley and its village life.

Introductions over, we had now reached the rollers at Iffley Lock. Here, we alighted and carried the canoe across to the other side. Only the heavier craft, like punts and rowing boats, used the rollers.

On the way downstream we caught a glimpse of the beautiful old Norman church. Its tower, nestling among the trees, made a most magnificent sight. Knowing how interested Americans are in ancient buildings, I took the opportunity of explaining in some detail the history of this wonderful church.

By this time we had reached an ideal spot in which to pull in, and after lifting the boat onto the bank, we sat down to enjoy the lovely scenery and wildlife to be seen in this part of the Thames. We watched the moor hens as they darted in and out of the weeds. A huge rat, disturbed by a passing steamer, scurried to the safety of the bank. Two swans fluttered their wings on the water as they prepared to take off to another part of the river.

It was at this point that Morgan suggested we had something to eat. This, I thought strange, until he explained he did not take lunch, but preferred a snack before dinner. The snack turned out to be a large cream and jam sandwich. This, to me, after the war years was a real luxury, and I certainly did justice to it. Even so, a large portion was left. This he carefully replaced back in the box. I could not help wondering what he would do with it. However, when we parted he handed the carton to me saying, 'This is for you to eat later in the evening.' I am sure he must have thought I looked hungry! Our first meeting did not end there, he wanted me to meet him the next day.

On reaching home I told my mother of our meeting, and explained about the cream sandwich.

'Do try some mother,' I said, 'It's lovely.'

She was a little wary at first remarking, 'You should not accept things from strangers.'

I explained that to me he was no stranger. He had behaved like a perfect gentleman. This seemed to reassure her, for she expressed no further concern when she knew I was meeting him the following day.

On the next afternoon, as I walked across the meadow, I could see him waiting by the side of the river. On seeing me, he waved, and came towards me. When we met, he held both my hands in a gentle embrace. Not being used to this kind of greeting, I blushed deeply. Seeing my embarrassment he smiled, and taking my arm, escorted me through the long grass to where the boat was moored. As we cruised gently along, he asked if I was interested in poetry? On learning that I was, he handed me a book of Omar Khayyam's poems.

He asked if I had read it. I had to confess I had never heard of it. As I glanced through the book, I noticed there were seventy-five verses, each one on a separate page. This to me was an entirely different layout of a poem and I expressed my surprise. He explained that Omar Khayyam was a Persian poet whose views were based on Fate, Freewill, Existence and Annihilation. He asked if I would like him to read some of his favourite verses. As he recited, I listened enchanted by the words and the way in which he expressed them. Often, in trying to fathom the true meaning of the words, he would repeat a verse several times. When he came to verse XXI, he said this was his favourite. He asked if I would recite it for him.

The words still stand out in my memory:

> Ah, my Beloved, fill the Cup that clears
> Today of past Regrets and Future Fears:
> Tomorrow! – Why, Tomorrow I may be
> Myself with Yesterday's Sev'n thousand Years.

In the week that followed we met each afternoon. Our conversation ranged from books to places of interest in this country and America. There was no doubt we had much in common. I felt I had always known him, he was so open. He spoke of his work with the Geological Oil Corporation, how it took him to far off places such as Mexico, Texas and Morocco. It was a lonely life and one that meant being away from home for long periods. I wondered why had was telling me this. Suddenly he took me in his arms and softly whispered, 'I love you!' As we lay in that fond embrace I looked into the eyes of a man whose respect and trust was beyond my understanding. As I slowly came back to reality I realised he was speaking of marriage, and what it meant to him. He said his work entailed living many months of the year away from civilisation as we knew it. He did not consider it right to become interested in a woman and then not be able to marry her. Marriage to him meant sharing a life together.

What could I say when I knew this to be true. My face must

have expressed my feelings, for it was then that he said, 'Don't be sad, Florence, it doesn't suit you.'

On our way back we said little to each other, both being occupied with our thoughts. It was not until he escorted me across the meadow that he voiced what I had been expecting, yet dreading to hear. In three days' time he would be returning to the States. We said no more. Our days together were numbered.

As I wended my way home, I tried to reason what it meant. Just a few more days. Would I lose him forever? Could fate be so cruel?

It was to my mother that I went for comfort and understanding. She meant so much to me, we had no secrets. She understood, and did her best to console me in what she knew was my first awakening of love.

Morgan Roberts' home at 2416 E. Third Street, Superior, Wisconsin, USA. He had two sisters and one brother. His work with the Geological Oil Corporation took him to Mexico, Texas and Morocco and he was away from home for long periods. In 1924 he was in Mexico living for three months in a bamboo hut. He had Indian help in the camp. They were very short people, but they were good workers.

This photograph of myself and Jimmie Farquharson, a Canadian, was taken at Sandford-on-Thames in 1919.

The next few days were the happiest, yet saddest days of my life. As I ticked each one off in my diary, I realised tomorrow would be our last day together. As I laid in bed, my thoughts in a turmoil, I could not sleep. It was then that I decided to write a full account of our meeting in my diary.

I remembered he had promised to give me a book of Omar Khayyam's poems. What could I give him as a parting gift? I had no money to buy a book. Suddenly I remembered I had won a book of poems as a prize when I was at school. It was entitled *Golden Treasury* and contained many of the poems that we were conversant with. I would give him this, knowing he would treasure it as I had done.

The weather was gorgeous as we met, on what was to be our last day together. He was leaving at nine o'clock the following morning, far too early for me to see him off at the station. We exchanged gifts, his book of Omar's poems. I have it still, with the inscription inside 'To my dear little Flo, from Morgan, Oxford, 1919'.

At last, it was time for us to say goodbye. That parting I shall never forget. His last words, 'Till we meet again,' then he was gone, and I was left wondering.

A few weeks after we parted I received my first letter. He had arrived home safely and was spending a short vacation before returning to his work with the Oil Corporation. He enclosed two photographs, one that he had taken of me before leaving England.

On the back he had written the verse:

> Drink to me only with thine eyes
> And I will pledge with mine,
> Or leave a kiss within the cup
> And I'll not ask for wine;
> The thirst that from the soul doth rise
> Doth ask a drink divine.
> But might I of Jove's nectar sip
> I would not change for thine.

The other photograph was of himself taken in his study and showing in the background my *Golden Treasury* in his bookcase.

Ours was a romance that was to last until his death in 1942.

The young men I met always seemed to be on the serious side. There was Jimmie Farquharson, a Canadian. He was a cadet in the Royal Flying Corps, stationed at Port Meadow, Oxford. We walked out together for about six months until he was transferred to a camp near Cirencester. Here, I visited him and stayed for two nights at the Fleece Hotel prior to his departure to Vancouver for demobilisation. On the morning he left I was having breakfast alone in the hotel dining room when I was joined by a middle aged Canadian couple who had previously shown a great deal of interest in us. They wanted to know if I would be coming to Canada to get married and if so, they would love to meet us. We exchanged addresses, but although Jimmie and I were extremely fond of each other, I knew I could never leave England while my mother was alive. We did, however, correspond until my marriage.

Then there was Walter Hockings, an officer, whose parents lived in Winchester. He became very serious. I remember we attended a service at Iffley Church. Afterwards we walked through the village hand in hand. In those days to be seen walking out with a man was thought to signify marriage. My father, who had seen us in the church together, was at home when I returned. He wanted to know who he was and what his intentions were. I explained he was only a friend.

However, I had reckoned without Walter, for when next we met he said he would like to meet my people, as he called them. It was then that I realised he really was serious. Not wishing to hurt him, I waited until I reached home, before writing to explain my thoughts and suggested that under the circumstances I thought I advisable not to meet again.

There were others less serious, like a captain I met whilst I was a waitress at Somerville Hospital. He was in the Royal Army Medical Corps. He invited me to have a drink with him. I recall we went to Buols in Cornmarket Street. Here I had my first liqueur.

Not knowing the names of any he read from the list, I accepted the last named, which was a creme de menthe. I liked it so much

My fiancé was stationed in Italy during World War I. He acted as interpreter for his Commanding Officer.

that I needed no persuading when he asked me to have another. It was not until I got into the open air that everything seemed to spin around. I remember he suggested a taxi to take me home. So, taking my arm, we walked to the taxi rank in Broad Street where he paid the driver, and saw me as he thought safely in to the taxi. I sat, as I thought, with my back to the driver, but in so doing, I had forgotten to pull down the seat and landed with a terrific bump on the floor. The driver appeared to take no notice, so I scrambled across the other side, and managed to find a seat. On reaching home, I went quickly to bed, but not to sleep. The bed seemed to spin round and round. It was my first and last liqueur. Next day when I met him at Somerville, he said he

I was married to Hubert Arthur George Wood, aged 29, on the 18th April 1921. He was born on the 1st November 1891 in Oxford and his father's name was Arthur William Wood who was independent. Witnesses were Percy W. Hine, Alice Kirby, my sister, and Richard William Kirby, my father. We were married by the Revd Owen S. E. Clarendon, Vicar of Iffley.

had been deeply concerned, and suggested in future we keep to tea and cakes.

Later, in 1919, I met my husband to be. We were introduced at a party, where I gathered he was home on leave from Italy. He explained that although the war was over, he was returning for a short period at the request of his Commanding Officer, to act as interpreter, mostly at social gatherings. We spent most of his leave together and on his return to Italy, corresponded regularly. It was during this period that he proposed marriage and, on his return, we became engaged. The saying 'distance makes the heart grow fonder' was, in my two real courtships, very true. My fiancé was in Italy and Morgan was in America. In both cases we were separated by sea, with only letters to bridge the gap. To me, these conveyed much more than the spoken word could ever hope to achieve.

I remember having to write and inform Morgan of our impending marriage. His reply was full of advice and also misgivings. That our meeting had awakened thoughts in me that would withstand actual marriage with another was beyond his understanding.

'You were so even tempered' he wrote. 'Make allowances for any shortcomings your husband to be may have – we men have

The best man, Percy W. Hine and bridesmaids. Sister Alice on right. My husband's father was born on the 29th September 1853 in Southsea and his grandfather on the 7th February 1802 in Guernsey, being privately baptised on the 7th March following at the Town church, St Peter Port, Guernsey, Channel Islands. His name was Henry Thomas Wood, son of Frederick Augustus Wood and Mary Dell, his wife. No records exist in Guernsey of their marriage.

many. Keep nothing from your husband. He should not deny either of us the pleasure of writing to each other.' I showed all his letters to my husband when we were married. They were so full of interest to us both.

Shortly before my marriage I received a letter from Morgan stating he was in England and staying at an hotel in London, on route to Morocco for the Oil Corporation. I phoned his hotel. Unfortunately he was out. This being so I asked my fiancé if I could call and see him in London. His reply was, 'If you do, our engagement is off.' I often wonder what would have happened had we met. I'm sure at that time I was in love with both men. I know my mother shared my secret.

Before my fiancé returned to Italy, he took me to meet his parents who lived in Wellington Square, Oxford. Apparently his father and grandfather had both been well known dancing masters. I gathered their main teaching had been to members of the University and their friends. Private parties for these were held in Wellington Square.

I still have a letter dated 28 April 1882, stating that His Royal Highness and friends will come to dance at 2.30 p.m. today, Saturday. (Signed) Yours truly, C. T. Ramsay.

His father also gave private tuition to local tradespeople, among them being W. P. Morris (later Lord Nuffield).

Apart from this he held regular dances at the Forum Restaurant in The High and also in a room at Taphouses in Magdalen Street, Oxford.

This was a time when presentations at Court were much in being, during which period he was kept busy with débutantes who came to practise the curtsy before being presented at Court. For this his fee was one guinea (21 shillings).

I gathered it was not until after the Great War that he finally decided to retire from his profession. This started with the death of Queen Victoria and later King Edward VII, each followed by six months Court mourning, when all forms of entertainment connected with the University were cancelled. He survived that, but after the Great War, dancing as he knew it had completely changed.

Gone was the graceful dancing of the ballroom, when ladies wore beautiful gowns, long gloves, and carried printed dance cards with pencils attached, for gentlemen to put their initials against the dance they wished to reserve. I gathered many of his friends tried to persuade him to carry on, but this would have meant going to London to learn the new dances, which, in any case he disliked. So he sadly decided to retire from a profession that had been in his family for two generations.

After this he came to live in Highfield, Headington, Oxford. After my marriage I met many people who said that never again would there be dances like those held by Mr Wood.

My husband came from a musical family. His parents were both very musical, his mother played the piano and his father the violin, not as customarily held under the chin, but in between the legs. My husband played the piano, violin, banjo and mandolin.

Now I spent a few months preparing for my marriage. At the time of my engagement I was apprenticed to hairdressing at a high class salon in Magdalen Street. My wage whilst learning was 2s. 6d. a week (12½p). It was an interesting experience and one, which at the time, I had hoped to take up seriously with the idea of opening up my own salon after marriage.

I was married to Hubert Arthur George Wood on 18 April 1921. I was twenty and my husband twenty-nine years old. The wedding was at Iffley Church. I wore a grey satin gown veiled with ninon and trimmed with seed pearls. Percy Hine was best man.

The two bridesmaids, Miss Alice Kirby and Miss Dorothy Woodward, wore beige dresses.

The Revd Owen S. E. Clarendon performed the ceremony. It was a beautiful service. The organist played the wedding march and the bells rang out.

I remember it was a cold spring morning and as we emerged from the church we were met with a blinding snowstorm. Fortunately someone covered us with a large umbrella and escorted us down the long churchyard path to our waiting taxi.

The wedding breakfast was held at the Tree Hotel, Iffley. It was a lovely reception. My dad had really gone all out to make it a day to be remembered. On a sideboard stood a beautiful three-tier wedding cake, a gift from my Aunt Bessie. There were twenty guests, excluding relatives. When we first arrived at the hotel it was to be greeted with a lovely coal and log fire. But, alas, owing to the coal strike, this was short-lived and when we left, only a few embers remained.

Not content with the coal strike, we arrived at Oxford Station to be met by the stationmaster, who informed us that owing to the pending rail strike, he was unable to guarantee any rail travel further than Reading. This being so, and with no time to make alternative arrangements, we decided to cancel our previous booking at Brighton and spend our honeymoon at Reading. Fortunately we both knew Reading well and as the train was already in the station we thought we could safely leave the booking of an hotel room until we arrived. Alas, this was not the case. Having called at two hotels and been met with excuses such as we are full up or the decorators are in, we stood in the drizzling rain and wondered what to do. Was it because of my youth? Or maybe they thought we were not married.

My husband suggested that at the next hotel he would go in alone and try to book a room while I waited outside. This succeeded, although when they saw me, their faces denoted disapproval.

However, we were shown to a room where we unpacked and dressed for dinner. Then, carefully collecting any rice or confetti from the carpet, we went to dinner. After dinner we were very surprised when the manageress came and congratulated us and hoped we would enjoy our stay in Reading. It was then that she explained. Most hoteliers would not let their room to couples unless a previous booking had been made.

At this point we thought it time to explain why we were at

My husband with the banjo. When living in Lime Walk, Headington, Oxford, people would stand outside the house to listen to the music.

Reading without booking. Having cleared this up it was drinks all round and the remainder of our stay was made as happy as possible.

When we returned to our room we wondered how she knew we were a married couple. It was then we discovered we had failed to notice some confetti had been caught up in the veil of a pretty navy blue togue I had been wearing when I arrived and had fallen onto the wardrobe shelf.

So ended our first day of married life, a day in which I had all my trials and tribulations, together with the snowstorm, the coal strike and pending rail strike. Then no accommodation available and standing in the rain, waiting to be admitted, more like a criminal than a bride. Not exactly a happy start to married life.

My husband's father,
Mr Arthur Wood,
1907 after catching a
large fish.

Once again, that nagging thought – was I right in having got married so young, and to a man I hardly knew?

After my marriage I continued to correspond with Morgan Roberts until World War II. In his last letter to me in 1939 he wrote, I cannot bear the thought of yet another war, or to think how long it will last. The heat here is terrific (Mexico) and I feel I cannot stand it much longer. Our letters will have to wait until after the war. My thoughts are with you. Think of me sometimes and try to understand what you mean to me. God bless you! Alas, this was to be his last letter, for after the war his sister wrote to inform me he had died of a heart attack in 1942.

So ended a romance that had lasted some twenty-three years.

For the first six years of our marriage we lived with my husband's parents at Lime Walk, Headington, an isolated spot off the main London Road. At that time the White Horse public house was the only building between Lime Walk and St Clements.

Being a country lover, my new surroundings were much to my liking. There were copses and beautiful country walks to Elsfield and Shotover Plain, over which, in the olden days, the stagecoach went on its way to London. Now it's a well-known beauty spot.

Then there was Marston Common and Stowe Wood, both renowned for rare butterflies and moths. My husband was very interested in these and had a wonderful collection. Like his father, he also loved fishing, a sport in which I soon became interested.

I gathered they used worms for bait and these had to be a certain kind, pinkish in colour and not too large. These were dug from the garden on the morning we went fishing. In dry weather the ground was well watered overnight and covered with a wet sack. This was removed in the morning, showing all the worms had come to the top.

The weather too played a great part. His father would never fish in an east wind, or when the water was low and sluggish. We always fished at a lovely isolated part of the River Thames near Kings Weir, this being a part not disturbed by steamers or too much boating.

The men had good fishing tackle and rods, but mine was a wooden rod with three joints. I would never touch a worm, so on my first day's fishing, my rod was the first to be fixed up and baited. I was then shown where to fish in what his father said was a perch hole. Much to their disgust, I caught two sizeable perch before they could even fix up their rods. I was terrified of pike, they always darted all over the river, finally taking the line into the reeds and usually the hook with it.

If possible I preferred to fish in a stream, some distance from the river. It was clear and shallow, with a low bank.

I remember on one occasion I caught a large chub. It had been basking in the sun and, until it moved, I thought it was part of a tree trunk. Fortunately it took the bait and I hooked it nicely and was able to drag it onto the bank. My shrieks of delight brought two gentlemen from their fishing higher up. They said I had frightened all the fish away, but they thought it was a fine fish.

Horse racing was another sport of my husband's father that I soon understood. He studied the horses and I studied the jockeys. My bet, a shilling each way, was taken to the bookmakers and often came up. This occurred so often that the bookmaker himself started to bet on my tips and my husband's father copied him.

6

Post World War I

Aftter the war I had no wish to return to domestic service. Five years of war had changed my entire outlook on life, I had grown from childhood to womanhood. Although only seventeen, I was determined to try and make my own way in the world. So I answered an advert in the *News of the World* for a barmaid at Highgate in London.

It was not until I received a letter to say my application had been accepted that I began to have misgivings. After all, it would be the first time I had left the village of Iffley or even travelled on a train. However, I arrived safely at my destination. It was a large corner building and looked quite impressive from the outside. The side door marked Private was opened by a woman who I afterwards discovered was the landlady. She showed me to the bedroom that I was to share with the other barmaid – her name was Maggie, a short Welsh girl. Maggie told me the family consisted of Mr and Mrs Cooper and their two daughters aged about eight and ten. According to Maggie, Mr Cooper was a hard man only recently demobbed from the forces.

On my arrival I was told to report at the bar one hour before opening time, when the landlord would be available to show me round. He was a tall thick set man, dark hair and with a deep voice more like a foghorn. When we met there was no formal greeting, but straight to business.

Firstly I was taken to study the price list, secondly to be shown the pumps and how to work them and thirdly when serving told to be sure to wait for the froth to go down, otherwise the customer would complain of short measure. On the other hand, don't waste it by letting too much go down the sink. As expected, on the

Myself aged seventeen.

first night one customer, on seeing a new girl, complained of short measure. This was soon rectified by the landlord coming along and filling it up himself. After this he continued to keep a watchful eye on me and when another man complained, the landlord accused him of having already drank some. After the first evening I became more assured and soon got into the way of serving.

Time off was not too bad. It consisted of most afternoons from 3–4 p.m. with an occasional afternoon and evening off until 10 p.m.

As my afternoons were spent in and around the nearby parks, I got to know this part of London very well so by the time my afternoon and evening off became due, I felt safe to visit the City. Here I was horrified to see the havoc caused by Kaiser Bill's recent bombing. To me it was unbelievable that anyone could have survived. After this I visited some of the shops. In the evening I had a late tea and having bought some sandwiches to eat on my return, I slowly wended my way back in time to reach the pub by 10 p.m.

Maggie was very pleased to hear I had followed her instructions and interested to know how I had spent my first day off. After this I began to find life much easier.

I also found that as I got to know the regular customers, so my work in the bar greatly improved. This, together with my visits to the City, became most enjoyable. Then on one particular night when I returned at the usual time of 10 p.m. I found I could get no reply to my repeated knocks and ringing of the bell. This was unusual. I was just beginning to get alarmed when a woman customer who I knew by sight, stopped to enquire what the trouble was. I explained the landlord would not open the door. She waited whilst I rang and knocked several more times, all to no avail.

'What can I do?' I asked.

Seeing my distress she said, 'You can't stay here all night. I live at the bottom of the road and if you don't mind sharing my room, you can stay the night with me.'

This could have been a calamity, but having no one to help me, I readily accepted her invitation. When we arrived she made me a hot drink with true Cockney kindness. Then, while I ate my sandwiches, she told me this was not the first time he had treated his staff this way, for no apparent reason. She then showed me to her bedroom where there were two single beds. When she said she would be sleeping in the other bed, I felt more assured.

After a sleepless night, she kindly gave me some breakfast and then escorted me to the pub to try again. However as he still refused to open the door, she advised me to go to the police. Then, having shown me the way to the police station, she left me and went on her own business.

When at last I reached the police station I entered, and with tears running down my cheeks, explained what had happened. I could not have received more kindness, as a policeman was called to escort me to the end of the road, then telling me to wait around the corner, he went alone to the pub. This time the door was opened and as the landlord still would not take me back, or give any reason for not doing so, the policeman asked for my luggage and also any money due to me.

I shall never forget his kind words as he called a taxi and seeing me and my luggage safely in, he leant over saying, 'Go home, my dear, London's no place for you!'

With no time to notify my mother of my homecoming, I arrived back to find my mother ironing in the same old room that I knew and loved so well. This was indeed 'Home sweet Home'. With my mother's arms around me I was too overcome for words. When at last I was able to pour out my sad tale of woe, my mother could hardly believe how a man with children of his own could be so cruel.

When my father came home we had a hard job to deter him

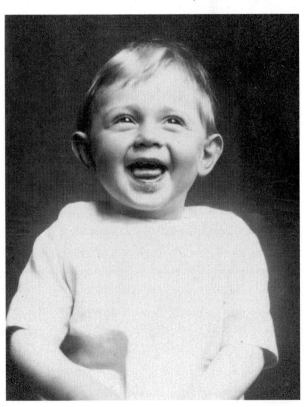

My son, Hubert Lionel, later to be in the RAF Regiment in 1942. He served in Norway from May 1945 and Palestine in 1946.

My son in the RAF Regiment in 1942.

from going to London to meet this man face to face as he said. 'You will do no good,' said mother. 'The policeman was right when he said London was no place for her.' However, father not to be outdone, finally wrote a letter to the landlord. We did not have any idea of its content, but at least it seemed to relieve his feelings.

In 1922 my son was born. He was a lovely baby weighing 8½lbs. Before his birth, we had already decided, if a boy, we would call him Hubert Lionel.

In 1928, when my son was six years old, we moved from Lime Walk to 232 London Road. It was a new semi-detached house

*Jimmie James, one of
our University
Graduates.*

built for sale by the council. A service road separated us from the main London Road and made for a very pleasant outlook. The house cost £900 freehold. My husband paid a small deposit from money left him by his aunt. The remainder we paid in monthly instalments to the city council at 5 per cent interest. To buy a house in those days was a big undertaking. I remember after the down payment, we were left with a monthly repayment of £12 with interest running at £18. Shortly after the council sold out to the Burnley Building Society and they reduced the interest to 4½ per cent. Even so, it took us twenty years to pay off the mortgage, during which there were no holidays and little social life.

When we first moved in Lionel was a pupil at the Field School, a church school on the London Road just past the crossroads at Headington, where I was later to become a governor. Later we paid for his education at Latham's Preparatory School, Banbury

Road, Oxford, and at the Oxford High School for boys in George Street, Oxford.

To help pay for the house and for schooling, we took in University Students. The first of these was a Mr Campbell. After being with us for a short period he was taken ill and he sent for the doctor. The doctor, Dr Stobie, went to 232 London Road, which was further up the road, near to London Road Hospital. It was then that he discovered there were two houses of the same address. Not only our house was involved, but the whole of the houses on the service road had duplicate numbers further up the road.

The doctor was furious and he contacted the city council. The London Road between Marston Road and the White Horse public house was then renamed Headington Road.

Before the First World War undergraduates were referred to as moneyed gentlemen. Even so, they would run up bills in Oxford,

Myself showing the building of Headington School.

Headington School in the 1990s. Photograph: Denis Kennedy

Headington School was founded in 1915 as a day and boarding school for girls, in order to provide 'the best possible spiritual, mental and physical education' (according to the first prospectus). By 1929, numbers had grown sufficiently for a new school to be built, which was opened by HRH Princess Mary, Countess of Harewood on 21st June 1930. Princess Mary said 'This will ever be to me a most memorable day, in which I have first of all received a degree from the University and secondly opened these very beautiful school buildings'.

In the mid-1980s, two wings were added on either side. The Science Block forms the east wing and is similar in style to Gilbert T. Gardner's 1930s main building. Its foundation stone was laid by Baroness Young in 1985. Later in 1989, the west wing was completed, housing the library, language and teaching rooms.

Headington is still thriving today and has become one of the leading academic schools in the country. There are over 600 pupils in the senior school, whose past pupils include Lady Elizabeth Longford, Baroness Young of Farnworth, Christina Onassis and newsreader Julia Somerville.

especially with their tailors, who, knowing their parents would pay, allowed them to do so. College dances were held on the last night of Eights week. Undergraduates were up at Oxford for three years. College Servants were much respected – staircase servants were known as scouts. Then there were College Butlers, Head Porters and second porters.

The long vacation was not good for people working at the colleges. Visitors did not come as they do today. Conferences in the colleges were unheard of. When not living in college, under-graduates lived in licensed lodging houses. The University was very strict about the licensing procedure and the University auth-orities visited all houses before granting a license.

Once, during Eights week, I helped to serve refreshments in one of the boathouses. The sun was shining from a cloudless sky, there were enchanting hats, hatted young men, mothers, fathers and sisters.

When Great Tom in Christ Church tolled a hundred-and-one times, one could see undergrads running to reach their colleges, as when the last stroke sounded all colleges shut their gates for the night. Anyone late had to pay a fine.

On 30 June 1969 Great Tom tolled 101 times when the Dean of Christ Church died.

Oxford Services Club Invitation from the United States Ambassadress. I worked as Supervisor at the Services Club until it closed down after the war. I usually finished about 10.30 p.m. However, the Army and Air Force personnel found it very useful when visiting Oxford from the surrounding bases.

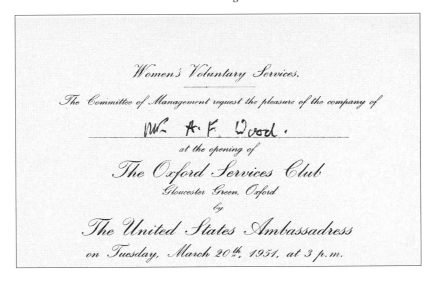

View from Cupola of Sheldonian Theatre.

Adjoining the Radcliffe Camera is the spire of the University Church of St Mary-the-Virgin.
The Radcliffe Camera is now part of the Bodleian Library. It was completed by 1749 and was
originally known as the Physic Library until 1861 when the Radcliffe library collection was
transferred to the University Museum. The Church of St Mary-the-Virgin was built in the
latter part of the fifteenth century on the site of an ancient Saxon Church. Cardinal Newman
was formerly Vicar of St Mary's, 1823–43.

As I walked through Iffley Village in the 1980s I see the village pubs have been brought up to date, but many of the old cottages remain. The fields and farmland have disappeared and bungalows for old people have been built. The old shop has become the general store and the butcher's shop now combines the sub post office. The school has gone. The quiet old churchyard is no more, children romp between the tombstones and graves. As I walk along the pathway to the Church, I note the untidy churchyard.

There are no children running home from school. All the people I meet are strangers to me. On my way back I walk down memory lane. Our cottage is still there, but it has been enlarged and there is no apple tree. The beautiful meadows have been covered in ballast to stop the flooding and the brook has been piped.

High Street showing two AEC Regent buses owned by the City of Oxford Motor Services Limited which were in service by 1932. Major Dixon was the General Manager of the company. Parcels were carried on country routes which had extended to Aylesbury, Banbury, Bicester, Chipping Norton, Faringdon, Henley, High Wycombe, Wallingford, Wantage and Witney. Later, services were run to Bedford, Newbury, Reading, Stratford-upon-Avon and Swindon.

The company became a subsidiary of the National Bus Company from 1 January 1969. This was the largest organisation of its kind in the world. By 1980 some long distance services were reaching Birmingham, Coventry, London, Northampton, Southampton and Worcester. Each Saturday a service ran to Weston-super-Mare via Bristol.

The City of Oxford Motor Services Limited was bought by the management on 15 January 1987 and by 1988 the National Bus Company had ceased to exist. Long distance services were gradually taken over by other operators although frequent services to London, Heathrow and Gatwick were retained.

Subsequently Grandforce Ltd. became the new owner in October 1990 and the Go-ahead Northern Bus Group purchased the Oxford Bus Company in March 1994.

Magdalen Bridge with Morris Cars of the early 1930s. All the trees on the left have been taken down. Beyond the bridge on the left hand side is now a Rose Garden and leading from the Rose Garden is the Botanical Garden. This was founded by the Earl of Danby in 1621. Occupying about five acres of ground it is one of the oldest instiutions of its kind in the country.

The River Thames, known locally as the Isis. All the College Barges have been destroyed and replaced by buildings. They were floating club houses for the members of College boat clubs. From this point to Iffley is the racing course where the summer 'Eights' and 'Torpids' are rowed.

Merton College Tower completed in 1450. Sheep no longer graze in this part of Christ Church meadow. A road was proposed to run across the meadow to alleviate traffic congestion in High Street. This was extensively debated by Oxford City Council, but was eventually rejected.

Magdalen College. This really is the most beautiful college in Oxford. It has a huge deer park and its Water Walks, which adjoin the shady River Cherwell, are well known. It was completed by 1504 on the site of the Hospital of St John. If the college grounds are included, it occupies well over 100 acres.

A corner in Oxford.

Tom Tower, Christ Church.

Beyond Tom Tower is the Great Quadrangle which is the largest in Oxford. On the east side is the West entrance to the Cathedral Church of Christ, which is also the Chapel of Christ Church. Although it is one of the smallest English Cathedrals, it is also the most attractive and enchanting. Christ Church is a collegiate foundation and is known within as 'The House'.

7

Illness

In 1954, when I was aged 53, I was not feeling too well. My son, who at that time was the Registrar of Births and Deaths for Oxford, persuaded me to go and see my doctor for a check-up. I went and came back with a note to go and see a specialist at the Radcliffe Infirmary. A doctor examined me and wanted me to go into hospital on the following Friday.

Not having had an illness before, I was not unduly troubled, although my husband and son, and indeed many of my friends, all seemed to know the nature of my illness, I seemed to be the last to know.

I remember writing a farewell note to my husband and son, telling them not to grieve if I did not come back, and to think only of the happy times we had spent together. This I put into my personal belongings marked '*Only* to be opened, should I not return.' With only three days in which to arrange helpers for the WVS Services Club, someone to bring the Club accounts to me each week, and helpers for the Children's Clothing Exchange, time passed very quickly. I then went into the Churchill Hospital, Headington, Oxford, on Friday, 19 March 1954.

After I entered hospital, I received a telegram of good wishes from the Chairman of WVS, Lady Reading. This was followed by a letter and a lovely little bed-jacket. I also received good wishes from both Headquarters and Regional Staff. These brought me great comfort and I remember the Sister saying, 'You must be a VIP, receiving all this attention.'

However, after a few days, sister came to my bedside and said 'You are going to have an injection.'

I knew no more until I woke later in the day. I remember

thinking, thank God that's over. It was not until next morning when sister came and removed some padding from me, that I knew it was some kind of treatment. I never felt nervous and if this was part of the care, put my faith in God and my surgeon.

The following morning I was up at 6 a.m. taking the early morning tea round to the other patients in the ward. 'Thought you had an operation yesterday,' said one. 'No,' I replied cheerfully, 'That was only treatment, I still have that pleasure in store.'

At night time I often went down and joined the nurses in a cup of tea. This little chat always refreshed me. On 22 March I received my first radium treatment. This was followed by the second treatment on 29 March, the third on 5 April and the fourth on the 12 April.

After the final dose I had radiation sickness all night, I really thought I was going to die.

I met one young person who had been in the hospital two weeks before I arrived and we discussed together our various feelings, especially after the treatment. She said, 'When having an X-ray, don't let them tip you upside down, I nearly passed out,' How grateful I was for this tip. I was able to say, 'Don't tip me or I shall faint,' and meant it.

When she was due for her final treatment, I woke up that morning and noticed her bed was empty. She had died in the night. The shock was awful. She had two young daughters still at school and her husband. She, herself, was young and attractive. Why, I asked myself, must this happen?

I remember there was also a lovely American lady in a bed the other side of the partition. At that time she used to make up beautifully. She must have known she was dying for she requested that her make-up be left on after death.

There was one poor woman in the bed next to me who apparently was always grumbling because the doctors could find nothing wrong with her. I think she really envied me especially when the sister brought the sleeping pills round and, as usual, I said, 'Not for me, thank you, Sister,' Not that I slept well, but I always had a dread of drugs of any kind, especially when sister said, 'Look at Mrs Wood, never a word of complaint.'

I then returned home on 29 April and was admitted to the Victoria ward at the Radcliffe Infirmary for an operation which was performed by Mr Stallworthy on 8 May to remove the womb, ovaries, and fallopian tubes.

Before my operation I was given a spinal injection and for some minutes, which seemed a lifetime, I was able to watch all the white-coated people crowding round as the gynaecologist prepared for the operation. Although I could watch all this, I felt no pain, and was presumably numbed from the waist down. I could hear the reassuring voice of my surgeon and my eyes slowly closed and I lapsed into oblivion.

After my operation, when I opened my eyes next morning I can remember hearing the voice of the only other occupant in the room saying, 'Thank God you are awake, all through the night matron and doctors have been coming in and out of the room.'

I remember watching the blood dripping into my arm. I thanked God that there were people in this world prepared to give their blood that we might live and wondered how many lives have been saved.

I looked across at the elderly lady, and she said that the doctors would not let her go home because she had no one to look after her.

Get well cards and flowers meant much to me. I prayed to God that my operation would be a success as there was so much in life that I wanted to do. Both my husband and son had prayed for me every night. Unless anyone has experienced this wonderful sense of knowing that all will be well, it is impossible to describe it. I am convinced that this wonderful understanding had much to do with the success of my operation.

On visiting days all patients were tucked up in bed and instructed to keep there until after visiting hours. Well, I always seemed to be given a sedative on those days which naturally always seemed to work during visiting hours. It became a standing joke, when no sooner did visiting hours start, than Mrs Wood had to literally run down the ward, much to the amusement of patients and visitors alike.

Later, when I was shown into the Day Room, I met four other patients. We soon got into conversation and I learnt they had been in hospital before. One motherly person was suffering from the same complaint. She asked if I knew why we were waiting. 'No,' I replied. It was then that she told me not to be frightened, we were going to be examined by students.

When I came out the same motherly person was waiting to comfort me. Putting her arms around me, she said, 'Don't upset yourself.' Having previously experienced the same examination herself, her words of comfort were like a ray of sunshine, for I had indeed found a friend. I must confess I had no idea the examination could be so painful.

Although during the four weeks I was in hospital, there was pain and suffering around me, I cannot describe the peace and calm that came to me in this time of trouble. Except for one's loved ones the outside world seemed so far away. Was it, I wondered, what I had been taught in my childhood – God helps those who help themselves.

While I was in hospital Lionel, my son, had shingles. How people keep their suffering from others. He hid this from me and continued to work, although he was in pain. I then went to a convalescent home.

I walked with considerable pain. I thought that my back would never straighten again, or the pain lessen. I understood this to be the result of the spinal injection.

Although still in pain I began my voluntary work once again, supervising the Services Club until it closed down a few years later. I then did the secretarial work in the WVS office, later being appointed to the Regional Staff in charge of National Savings for the Region.

After my operation I visited hospital every month, then every six months, after that once a year for six years. How happy I was when finally the doctor said, 'You need not come again,' I was always nervous during these visits.

During my time in hospital my husband had visited me regularly every afternoon. I wondered at this, but refrained from asking him.

It was during this time that my husband's health began to fail and when I came out of hospital, it became apparent to me. His health continued to deteriorate and after five years he died in 1960. Unfortunately he did not understand what was going on around him during this period.

During my time in hospital Freedom Forum, incorporating the Oxford Ratepayers' Association, which was non-party, asked me to stand for the City Council with the Revd R. Swinson. I was Chairman of the Oxford Branch. At that time it was said that the Housing Subsidy, a six shillings and sixpence rate only, was largely paid by ratepayers who had invested in a home of their own. It cost the country £100 million in rates and taxes. The City Council refused to recognise 'Self Build' housing schemes which made practically no charge on the rates. It was said that Oxford's debt was increasing at the rate of £800,000 a year and the annual interest payable amounted to £250,000. Freedom Forum stood for fair play for the individual and wanted representatives who had ratepayers' interests at heart. However, as I was still in hospital, I did not think it fair to stand for Freedom Forum. I did attend a conference at Brighton and a Captain Blunt took me down by car. He boasted a Veteran's badge on his car, but to my surprise his idiom was, 'If you're going to have an accident, hit them hard.' His speed alarmed me.

On the way back we called at a restaurant for tea. To my embarrassment instead of waiting for a waitress to take our order, he called out 'Hi Wench' to every waitress that passed by. 'Wait your turn,' was the only reply he got, but finally we were served. I was interested in his knowledge of tree names as he pointed out the chalk ring which denoted that the tree must come down.

8

The Women's Voluntary Service

WVS, as it was then called, first came into being in 1938 when Lady Reading, our Chairman, was asked by the then Home Secretary, Sir Samuel Hoare, to recruit women to help in the emergency of war, based on the pattern of the Civil Defence of the Local Authority, also to use women with only part time to spare for the national effort.

It showed much for Lady Reading's remarkable gift for leadership in that she was able to convince women that even if they only gave a few hours service a week, it would make an incalculable difference to the course of events. Starting with a membership of five, by the end of the first year WVS was 300,000 strong and by the end of the war, over a million strong. WVS work in those days covered canteen work, clothing, evacuation and billeting.

It was, I suppose, not surprising that in the post war period after the WVS experience in helping people in distress, we were asked by the Government of the day to help Local Authorities with Welfare Services.

In July 1966 we were honoured by HM the Queen with the title of 'Royal' because of our proved reliability and willingness to take responsibility. I think it is interesting to note that WRVS are members of a Service and not an Organisation. We have no badges denoting ranks, but it is the willingness to take responsibility that specialists in the different fields of work are chosen to be responsible for the day to day work.

WRVS held no funds in offices. Postage and telephone expenses were paid for from a grant by the Central Government. There were no salaries, but if a person of ability was unable to do the work, then a small amount of out of pocket expenses was allowed.

Lady Reading, our Chairman, founded the WVS and worked extremely hard to make it a success.

Profits from trolley shop services to hospitals were paid back to the hospitals in gifts of kind.

A volunteer to the Service signed a form stating the amount of time she was able to give and the procedure for earning her membership was sixty hours of service. She was also required to hear two talks, one on WRVS work and the other a One in Five Talk which informed women what to do in an emergency and what could be done to mitigate the effect if there should be a nuclear attack.

After 15 years' service of no fewer than forty duties per year there was a WRVS medal and after a further twelve years a bar was added. I received the Medal and Bar. WRVS worked in contact with the Local Authority Clerk of the Council, Medical Officer, Welfare Officer, Probation Officer and Ministry of Social Security, also through hospital authorities, local doctors and other organisations, such as Home Help and the Council of Social Service.

Welfare work included helping individuals and families to maintain independent lives in their own homes, also to provide amenities for those in hospitals or their own homes. We had over 2,000 Old People's Clubs, and in some areas these were all day Clubs, providing luncheons and teas. A chiropody service was also provided. WRVS had twenty-two residential homes for old people and three nursing homes under arrangements with the Ministry of Health.

WRVS had a Charitable Trust from legacies and gifts. Flats from this fund have been built in Winchester and also houses on the south coast for retired professional people, but as expected, a long waiting list for these existed.

In hospital welfare WRVS undertook non medical work in 1,450 hospital canteens in outpatients departments for visitors and patients; also shops and trolley shops, library services, escort duties and visiting patients who came from some distance and relatives had difficulty visiting them.

Much stress was laid on children's welfare, on preventative work to keep families together and thus avoid taking children into care. WRVS ran a holiday scheme for some 3,500 children and Mother and Baby Clubs. Help was also given in welfare clinics and looking after handicapped children.

Services welfare is not now carried on on such a large scale as in the past when specially trained and selected members were posted overseas to rest camps for troops; also welfare work with families overseas, particularly in Germany.

Collecting magazines entailed an adoption scheme and sending them to an adopted unit or NAAFI Club. In summer months the WRVS went with army Cadets and supervised and cooked meals for the boys at the camps. When large-scale exercises were held, we were called in to help with refreshments for the Royal Ordnance Corps. There was also an adoption scheme for refugees and £3 coal parcels.

Myself in WVS uniform. I was awarded the WVS medal and bar.

Many people still needed help with clothing so we collected and accepted offers, which were sorted, sized and tied in bundles of five according to their category and marked with their code number. Stocks were kept ready for emergencies, both for home and abroad. Bales for overseas were sent through the British Red Cross. Prison Welfare was an important job. Every night a member of the WRVS visited Holloway Jail and if a prisoner so wished, she could meet her and ask for help. Probably her family had no idea what had happened or there might have been a problem at home where help was needed. Local WRVS were then notified and arranged to visit the home. When they left prison they may have asked for a WRVS friend in their area who would then visit them during the first few months they were at home and try and help them over their problems, but no money was given.

Escorts were provided for wives of men serving sentences in

isolated prisons, also where girls were on home leave from Borstal or when being discharged. Canteens were run in prisons, remand homes and courts. Prisoners' luggage was collected and taken into the care of the Probation Officer. This was handed back when the prisoner was discharged.

When nuclear attack was considered likely, One in Five (one in five of the population) talks were given and this was one of the two talks necessary before a volunteer could become a member of WRVS. It was a talk based on how to protect your home and family, should there be a nuclear attack. The object was to bring this to the notice of 1 in 5 people in the country – hence its title.

The emergency training was to prepare people to work as a team, thereby knowing exactly what to do and so save valuable time. This covered a blanket pack, mouth to mouth resuscitation, clothing, emergency cooking, inquiry point and emergency home care.

Having covered WRVS work as a whole, I now come to children's holidays. Requests for these came through Health visitors

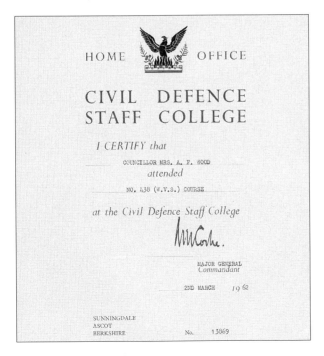

Certificate of attending the Civil Defence Staff College at Sunningdale.

The Civil Defence College at Sunningdale.

Group attending Sunningdale Civil Defence Staff College. Self, front row, fifth from left.

and the Children's Officer. Locally these included looking after children at the Lord Mayor's Party, Oxford, the lost children's tent at St Giles' Fair, Oxford, and outings to Wicksteed Park. Clothing was accepted at 9 Park End Street, Oxford, where there was an emergency stock and at the County Office, Alexandra Courts, Woodstock Road, Oxford.

There was a trolley shop at Cowley Road Hospital, Oxford, where proceeds were given back in kind. A library service was also provided together with the League of Friends, which was at River-mead Hospital, Oxford.

The Meals on Wheels Service used to be shared by the Red Cross being responsible for the delivery of meals to the east of Magdalen Bridge covering Marston, Headington, Cowley, Rose Hill and Iffley and WRVS covering St Clements, East Oxford, Iffley Road to Donnington Bridge Road, then through to South Oxford, West Oxford, Walton Street and North Oxford.

The Red Cross collected their meals from Marston Court and Iffley House Old Peoples Homes and WRVS from the Municipal Restaurant in St Clements. Meals were delivered in heated containers either by van or private car. WRVS meals were delivered by private cars. They were subsidised by the Local Authority and the old people paid 1s. 6d.

The value of the service was that it enabled elderly people to remain in their homes. Also WRVS members were able to keep a friendly eye on them and report back to the local WRVS office of any needs which they may notice. It may have been that a doctor or nurse should be notified, or the help required may have been simply helping them to write a letter or change a library book. This was, of course, greatly appreciated by the recipients, who were recommended by doctors, the Health and Welfare Department, district nurses, home helps and Medical Social Workers. There were four meals weekly.

There were eight clubs covering Old People's Welfare, two of which – in South Oxford and in St Ebbes' – celebrated twenty-one years since inception. These again formed a very strong link in that Leaders visited their members if they were ill or in hospital.

Old People's Holidays covered the Isle of Man, Llandudno and Eastbourne. Distance was no object. Day outings and visits to pantomimes were also enjoyed.

The WRVS were also responsible for helping the National Savings Movement. Many of our members were Street Group Secretaries. This side of National Savings included Social Groups and we were able to include our Old People's Clubs, who saved through stamps or through the Trustee Savings Bank and this came in useful for paying bills such as electricity, gas, radio and television licences. The amount saved could also cover holidays. Again, this form of personal contact was much appreciated. I worked closely in those days with Douglas Hurd, MP, for the National Savings Movement.

The Silver Jubilee of the WRVS was in 1963. The function of WRVS is to support, but never to direct completely. We were often asked to man Information Centres and one which stands out in my mind was Wimbledon, where I helped on three occasions and covered a fortnight every year. The only free thing we were allowed was a ticket on the centre court when off duty. Railway fares, hotel expenses, etc., were paid by members of WRVS attending.

Victory Parade, Saturday, 8 June 1946

I was one of 144 WVS members taking part. WVS was divided into twelve regions, this meant twelve from each region, ours being region six.

We all had to wear green uniform, hats, flat heeled shoes, and be capable of marching seven miles. We met at Reading where an army officer gave us instructions on how to stand at ease, attention, and of course, how to march. We had to bear in mind that although WVS was not a marching column, we were nevertheless taking part in a big parade and should not let WVS down.

The next day we went to London and met in Smith Square, where we were taken by cars to Chelsea Barracks. On the parade ground we were drilled by a Sergeant Major of the Irish Guards.

We were led by the pipes. Never in our wildest dreams had we expected so much glory. We swung along feeling magnificent, but all too soon the pipers had to depart. It was then that our Sergeant

Rehearsal at Chelsea barracks for the Victory Parade in 1946.

Major told us exactly what he thought. He called us Madam, but apart from this, there were no compliments. He did not say much, but we understand that as a marching column we were a pretty depressing spectacle. However there was no doubt from soldiers leaning from the windows, clapping and shouts of well done, they thought otherwise.

After two hours of practice we returned at 6 p.m. to be taken to the Thackeray Hotel, where we stayed the night. Here we thought we could rest until dinner, but no sooner had we removed our shoes, then an order came to proceed to the British Museum to have final instructions from a Sergeant of the Welsh Guards. Our marching earned us a 'well done' he, of course, having no idea we had just returned from Chelsea Barracks.

The seven-mile march went from Hyde Park up Whitehall and past the Cenotaph. It was wonderful in The Mall. Here we straightened up and our Officer moved up and down the lines to see if we were in step, all shoulder to shoulder. As we neared Saluting Base we could see out of the corner of our eyes the pageant ahead.

The Rehearsal

If I ask you most politely, and with masterly restraint,
To stand stiffly to attention and endeavor not to faint,
While I'm giving you instruction, not to giggle, talk or wink,
If I ask you, oh, so nicely, could you do it do you think?

If I ask you oh so gently, with no vestige of a frown,
Just to swing your arms most naturally, not to flap them up and
    down,
And I'd really be most grateful if you'd try to keep in line,
And not give an imitation of the ruddy Serpentine

Would you kindly throw your shoulders back? And please don't
    think me rude
If I say I have to wonder what you'd look like in the nude,
But you'd better make an effort, girls, no matter how you're made,
For you're meant to be rehearsing for the Victory Parade.

Now I'm sick of being nice to you, I think I've had enough;
You may be of the gentle sex, but I believe you're tough,
So turn about and wheel about and dress it by the right,
I'll see you have an ache or two when you go home to-night.

So left and right and left and right, and keep a steady line,
And keep your tummies in, my girls – come on, you're doing fine,
Why, if the King were standing now upon his Royal stand,
'E wouldn't 'arf be proud of you, the Mothers of his Land.

The Queen was in mauve, the Princesses in blue. There was Queen
Mary, the Duchess of Kent and Winston Churchill. Then it was
over when we came to Buckingham Palace. But we had one more
special thrill.

These were soldiers round Queen Victoria's statue and when
we came in view they shouted three cheers for WVS, thanks for
everything. This brought a lump into our throats and we stumbled
a bit as we went towards the dismissal point. It was raining. We
thanked our Officer.

He smiled, and then surprised us all by saying, 'I was proud of you.'

And how did we look to an onlooker?

From a balcony by the Church of St Martins-in-the-Fields I could see the curve of Charing Cross Road on my right and fountained, beflagged Trafalgar Square on my left. The crowds were huge. Our first big cheer came as the King and Queen and the Princesses drove by in that truly beautiful state landau, drawn by the Windsor Greys, and escorted by the clanking, jangling, sparkling Horse Guards. A great roar of praise rose up into the grey sky – it must have rocked the stars.

Much as I admire the WVS and believe it capable of all things, I must confess I did not expect it to march well. It is not designed for display, either physically or mentally.

When I saw that compact square of blurred green coming towards me from the distance, I felt that strange constricting of the heart and strangling of the throat which tokens love, but my brain nevertheless warned me not to expect more than two women in each row to be in step. But I was wrong – there they came from every part of Britain, marching perfectly in step, twelve abreast, not swinging their arms too high, looking straight ahead and keeping in line. I couldn't believe my eyes. I knew they had had one memorable drilling from a Guards sergeant, but either he had put the fear of God into them, or else they were otherwise celestially inspired. And whatever miracle of love persuaded them to wear their hats at the correct angle for once.

To the crowds who gave them a cheer they were just the dear old WVS, as familiar to their everyday life as a nice cup of tea, but to me they represented eight years measured in ranging degrees of sacrifice.

They were the mobile canteen standing at the corner of a burning Bristol street, the clothing depot working eighteen hours a day in Liverpool, the incident enquiry point set up on a pavement in Brixton and the evacuee train arriving in Wales.

They were the hurried housework in the morning, the long,

cold ride to work on a bicycle, the queuing for rations in the lunch hour, the race from the office to cook the evening meal.

They were the forms to be filled in, the layettes to be counted, the endless improvisation, the constant frustration, the utter fatigue. They were the bomb, the rocket, the stirrup pump. They were endurance, quietness, kindness.

Who shall blame me if my eyes rested on them more lovingly than on any other part of the procession, and if my heart followed them to the end of their journey, as indeed it always must?

The Roll of Honour was dedicated in Westminster Abbey by Her Majesty Queen Elizabeth on 20th November 1951, and after a three months' tour of the United Kingdom, during which it was on view in cathedrals, guildhalls and museums, it now rests in St Nicholas Chapel, Westminster Abbey. It may be seen by request at any time unless a service is being held. The Roll of Honour records the names and citations of 241 WVS members killed during the years 1939–45.

The work which took five years to complete, was produced by Miss Claire Evans who was a founder member of the Society of Scribes and Illuminators, one of the first members of the Council of the Crafts Centre of Great Britain and who joined WVS three days after war broke out. The Roll of Honour, inscribed on vellum, was bound by Mr R. Powell of the Royal College of Art in red morocco leather.

Illuminated panels show all aspects of WVS work during World War II. The colouring is offset with burnished gold, the work of Miss Irene Base.

9

Oxford City and Politics

Aфтер му маrriage I became interested in politics. I joined the local women's Conservative Club. Here, apart from various political speakers, we had a very good social side, including bridge, which I enjoyed. Later, when I became secretary of the club, it was suggested that I should take up public speaking, so I went to Swinton College, which was known as the Conservative College of the North. Here people trained for Parliament and local councils.

I passed my exams and although I did not become an MP, I did become a City Councillor. I was also appointed by Conservative Headquarters as a public speaker for the Southern Region.

In 1960 I was elected to Oxford City Council, a year in which I still have vivid memories of joy and sorrow. This started during my first year in office, when the Town Clerk informed me that the Queen and the Duke of Edinburgh would be visiting Oxford and the University and had expressed a wish to meet the Council. This meant lady members would have to practise their curtsy and the question of gloves was under discussion.

To me, this was a great thrill. When the great day arrived, one by one we mounted the stairs to the Town Hall stage and were duly presented in order of service to the Queen and the Duke of Edinburgh. Having just been elected, I was one of the last to be presented. The Queen smiled and shook hands, whilst the Duke, knowing I was a new member, asked if I was finding my way around, to which I replied, 'Yes, Sir.'

After the ceremony Council members lined the stairs as they left for their lunch at Christ Church. So ended a memorable day.

The sad news was in August of that year I lost my husband.

Oxford Old Folks New Years Party

(Founded 1936 by the late Alderman D. Oliver and the late
Alderman C. Brown)

PROGRAMME

OXFORD OLD FOLKS PARTY COMMITTEE

have pleasure in presenting an

ENTERTAINMENT BY

The City of Oxford Boy Scouts

and

Vera Legge's School of Dancing

in the

TOWN HALL, OXFORD

on

WEDNESDAY, 11th JANUARY, 1967

commencing 5.30 p.m. (approx.)

Programme 1/-   N⁰   2

Oxford Old Folk's Party Committee

In January each year 400 old age pensioners were given a meal followed by entertainment on Wednesday and a further 400 on Thursday. When leaving the Town Hall they were given a parcel containing fruit and groceries. The privileged classes. Sir, Mr Fenn's letter in last week's Oxford Times, asked who are the privileged classes? Who are they who are above our by-laws? The answer is for once in a way, the privileged classes were the old people of 70 years and over who had been attending their annual party at the Town Hall. The three buses in question had been lent by the bus company (free of charge) to convey old people to their homes in different parts of Oxford. In order to provide the maximum amount of safety for old people, the police kindly gave permission for the buses to park outside the Town Hall. Florence Wood (Mrs) (Hon. Secretary, Oxford Old Folk's Party Committee.)

But, life has to go on and I knew occupation of mind was a great healer.

I went into local government because I wanted to be better able to serve the city in which I lived. I also enjoyed meeting people and being able to do things for them. I had the time to give to it, which was all important. I also found a great need for women on the City Council. This was clearly shown by the number of people who came to me for help and advice. Whether the request was large or small, to the individual it was all important.

I remember one such case when calling on some of the people in my ward. The person invited me into her house as she had

---

Oxford & District
Women's Conservative Club

21 GEORGE STREET, OXFORD

(opposite New Theatre)

FIXTURE LIST - OCTOBER, 1951

OFFICERS.

President :
Viscountess Hailsham.

Chairman :
Alderman Lady Townsend, J.P.

Hon. Treasurer :
Councillor Mrs. M. Packford.

Hon. Secretary :
FLORENCE WOOD.

Assistant Hon. Secretary :
Mrs. E. West.

Oliver & Son, Printers, Oxford.

Fixture List for the Oxford & District Women's Conservative Club for October 1951.

something confidential to impart. It turned out she wanted me to intervene between her children and the next door neighbour's children, who according to her, when at school were always fighting with her children. I went to see the headmaster of the school. He knew of this particular trouble that existed between the two families and informed me that one family was from Northern Ireland and the other from Southern Ireland. So I went back to the mother without telling her where I had got the information from, and suggested that the two families get together, thereby showing the children that they were all friends. Then it all came out amidst a torrent of language. I could well imagine no reconciliation was possible and for my part, I beat a hasty retreat.

Although I was not able to do anything in this case, I do feel that this is one field in which women tend to have the advantage over men. For instance, having to run a home, women, I think, acquire a more practical outlook on questions involving children, the elderly and prices.

Myself when on
Oxford City Council.

Myself with Alderman Mrs Andrews, Alderman Meadows and Alderman Kinchin.

Group at Swinton College, known as the Conservative College of the North, where training was given for future councillors and members of parliament. Myself second row standing, sixth from the left.

The Civic Catering Association held their Annual General Meeting at the Winter Gardens, Malvern in March 1969. Some of those attending were Cllr W. W. Emerson, Hartlepool; Cllr C. Foster, Easington; Cllr J. R. McClure, Gateshead; Miss P. M. Cooper, Oxford: Cllr Mrs L. M. Burton, Lambeth; Mr J. P. Reynolds, Hartlepool; Cllr Mrs A. F. Wood, Oxford; and standing Mr K. Yould, Lyons Maid.

The White Rabbit Snack Bar when it was originally opened at Cowley Centre, now known as Templars Square, Oxford.

WHITE RABBIT SNACK BAR

POUND WAY, COWLEY CENTRE, OXFORD.

Prominently situated in a fine corner position in Pound Way the main pedestrian shopping thoroughfare from the larger of the two multi-storey car parks to the Central Square, close to the Banks and established offices.

Excellent modern purpose-built premises with all modern facilities.

Myself, Cllr for the South Ward, Oxford, and Alderman Mrs Andrews MBE who received the freedom of the City of Oxford. She was Mayor of Oxford in 1950–51.

I was on the Health Committee and found visiting Old People's Homes most rewarding. The old people looked forward to these monthly meetings, because apart from holding our Committee meeting at the Home, it gave us the opportunity to meet them and discuss their problems. If anything was wrong, we were able to take it up on their behalf.

When a new Home was built, the Committee sometimes spent two whole days going through samples of furniture and bedding, etc. All had to be tested for reliability and comfort. Then there was the type of curtains and what colour material to have. This was done by the ladies and sometimes when we agreed, we were told it was too expensive and we had to start all over again.

The Catering Committee, of which I was the Chairman, was responsible for four restaurants. This was an after war project and for some time they served a useful purpose. Now they have all been closed and houses and shops built on the land on which they once stood.

Left to right; Barbara Boddy, wife of Leslie Boddy, the City Mace Bearer; Myself; Alderman Mrs Florence Andrews MBE; and my son, Superintendent Registrar, Oxford, 1969.

Then there were special Committees such as the Cowley Centre Committee and the Central Area Redevelopment Committee. These were formed specially to deal with new projects too large for any existing Committee. Central Area was, in its early stages, a nightmare, covering as it did a wide field which entailed purchasing all leasehold and freehold properties where new development was needed to take place. This included space for a new library and shopping centre.

I think the worst part was when it came to the upheaval of people from their homes, people whose parents and grandparents had lived in the Friars all their lives. This was in my ward and I knew all these people personally. You can well imagine the heart-rending scenes that took place. I hope I never experience anything like it again. I often look at the grand new buildings and think of the wonderful community that once lived there.

Apart from Committee work, there were Church Services. These became so numerous we had to limit them to special occasions such as the Cenotaph Service and Lord Mayor's Carols.

On two occasions we attended prison services. I shall never forget when we entered the Chapel and the inmates, already assembled, stood up. The singing was wonderful and one wondered why they were there. It was a very moving experience.

In 1969 Council attended the St Frideswide Service at Christ Church when the new Dean was installed. Afterwards, South Ward Councillors had the honour to be invited by the Dean of Christ Church, to dinner at the High Table. However, there we were, Alderman Mrs Andrews and myself, seated between twenty-six dignitaries. To add to this the high table was lit up. Down in the body of the hall sat all the students in semi-darkness. It was so quiet down there that had you not known they were there, you would never have believed it possible.

Opening of Radio Oxford, 29 October 1970.

Radio Oxford on the air

The Lord Mayor, Ald. Michael Maclagan, recording his opening broadcast at Radio Oxford yesterday. In the background is Mr Donald Norbrook, Controller of Radio Oxford.

In his speech Ald. Maclagan said "Our City has known many noteworthy steps forward in its com-munications." He traced the history of communications in Oxford and added "today another revolution is at hand. This is a development I welcome most warmly on behalf of you all."

Radio Oxford opened at 5 p.m. yesterday when the Lord Mayor's speech was heard.

After dinner we adjourned to the Senior Common Room for dessert and drinks. As at dinner, our places were all marked out, but as the evening drew on, we intermixed a little and moved to different parts of the room.

Our most embarrassing moment was when Mrs Andrews and myself wanted to visit the toilet. Who could we ask? As we were not sitting together, we could only make signs. So at last I plucked up courage and asked the person sitting next to me. Of course, it meant he had to get up and take me along various corridors, then across a quad, until at last I arrived at the toilet. Whilst in there I thought I shall never find my way back, but to my great surprise my chaperon was waiting to take me back. On the way I met Mrs Andrews, also being escorted. However, we must have behaved ourselves as the Master of Pembroke, who was also attending, invited us at a later date to dinner at Pembroke College.

I forgot to tell you about the snuff box. This was handed round saying, 'Everyone who dines at Christ Church must take a pinch of snuff.' We were shown how to do this on the back of the hand.

I attended the Inspection of the City Walls, New College, on Wednesday, 9 May 1962.

The Programme was as follows:

10.45 a.m. Council assemble at Town hall for robing.

11.10 a.m. Council, preceded by Mace and City Marshal with Chief Constable's Mace, process to the main gate of New College via Catte Street and New College Lane.

11.30 a.m. Arrive main gate of New College which will be closed. City Marshal knocks (three raps) with handle of his Mace; the gate is fully opened by the College Porter; the City Marshal requests permission for the Mayor and City Council to enter and inspect the City Walls.
Permission being given, the procession enters and is greeted by the Warden (Sir William Hayter KCMG, MA) and Fellows of the College who will be immediately within the gate.

Continuing in procession, Council, led by the Warden and Fellows, will proceed via the Front Quadrangle to the Garden of the College where the inspection of the City Walls will take place – (ladder provided).

Members of the public will be admitted to the garden. By invitation of the Warden and Fellows, all members of Council attending the inspection are invited to join them for a little refreshment in the Founder's Library, and will doff their chains and robes in the Old Bursary en route.

After refreshment, members will disperse informally. Mayor's Sergeant to make arrangements for the collection of robes from the College Lodge during the afternoon.

If wet, transport will be standing by to take members from the Town Hall to New College – the actual inspection being curtailed as the weather demands.

Mayor's Parlour
Oxford
30 April 1962

St Giles' Fair

St Giles' Fair is the largest street fair in the country. It is held on the Monday and Tuesday after the first Sunday in September unless Sunday is the 1st of September, then it is held on the 9th and 10th of September.

The first mention of the Fair was in 1625. It is a Wake, that is a local annual festival of the parish, and therefore did not originate by Charter or Act of Parliament.

The Fair has been held continually except for war. An illustration of this was when World War II was declared in 1939, the fair was cancelled.

After the war the Markets and Fairs Committee who, acting on advice of the Chief Constable, asked Council to agree that the Fair should not be resumed in 1945 to enable the whole question of the resumption of the Fair in the future be dealt with at an

St Giles' Fair, Oxford, 1921. The fair extended the length of the broad thoroughfare of St Giles' and then divided into the Banbury and Woodstock Roads. the larger roundabouts were on the right of St Giles' with the smaller shows and switchbacks on the left. Due to the camber of the road, wooden blocks were placed under the roundabouts to level them.

Typical traction engine owned by W. Nichols who came to the fair each year.

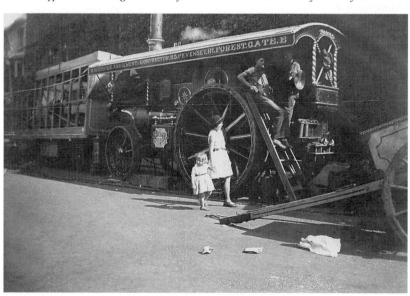

Stop me and buy one, Wall's Ice Cream showing the northern part of the fair.

early date. Fortunately this recommendation was rejected by Council which instructed the Fair should be held in 1945, and it has been held annually ever since.

Before World War II showmen were not allowed to enter St Giles' before 5 a.m. on the Monday and during the early part of the twentieth century no caravan was permitted to enter the Fair until an inspection by the Sanitary Inspector. The caravans were real showpieces with their polished brass and colourful wooden panels. The traction engines, which provided the electricity, shone to perfection. I have never ceased to marvel at the quickness of erection, every part being noted and quickly slotted into position. The Fairs Superintendent was responsible for marking the plots and many showpeople had the same plots each year. Special trains were run from as far away as Birmingham and by nightfall the Fair was usually completely full.

There were boxing booths, side shows, the cake walk and switchbacks. There was a menagerie, variety show and picture shows with dancing girls outside while the public went in. I remember going to see one of these films. It was a sea film and I was sitting in one of the cheapest seats. So crude were the films in those days that it seemed as though the waves were coming towards me, and I drew back in terror. There was always a fat woman and a living skeleton. Then there were the galloping horses, the big wheel and the helter-skelter. All the roundabouts had lovely organs which were beautifully illuminated. In the evening the Fair was ablaze with coloured lights.

For sentimental reasons I should be sorry to see the Fair abolished, although it retains little of its former glamour. Before World War II a ride on the roundabouts cost 3*d.* during the day and 6*d.* in the evening. All schools remained closed for the two days after the summer holidays. Pubs in St Giles' did a roaring trade.

In October 1957 the Watch Committee was once again asked by the Chief Constable to consider moving the Fair from St Giles' to another site. It was said that tradition is important and valuable, but against this had to be weighed the interference with trade and traffic.

However, at its meeting on 5 December 1957, the Markets and Fairs Committee indicated that the Watch Committee be informed that this Committee was unanimous in its opposition to the removal or abolition of the Fair.

I will always remember the General Election of 1938, when I had the opportunity to work with the Conservative candidate, the Hon. Quintin Hogg, later Lord Hailsham. At that time I was Chairman of the Headington Branch of the Conservative Party.

I remember we toured the City in a coach and four. On one occasion the Liberal party followed us round in a car. When we reached Walton Street they decided to return, thanking us for taking them round.

I replied, 'It's been a pleasure, we've been only too pleased to put you on the right road!'

Politics was fun in those days and parties were polite to one another. I had the pleasure of accompanying the candidate on his tour of hospitals and other public buildings.

Election Broadcasts

The first Radio Oxford Election broadcast took place in May 1971.
A note was given to all Councillors and Candidates who were to
take part. The following is an extract:

> Just before each Broadcast, you will be given the opportunity to
> meet the other Candidates and meet the Chairman of the
> discussion. At 7 p.m. a recorded broadcast by Ald. Michael
> Maclagan will describe the work of the Council, its composition
> and functions. A discussion between Candidates then followed.
> In the first Broadcast, one Candidate [the St Clements Liberal]
> persisted in pounding the table as he spoke. This may be
> effective on television, but on Radio all one hears is the
> speaker's voice, drowned by occasional thumps!
>
> If any Candidate wishes to light a cigarette during the
> discussion, it would be appreciated if they could only strike a
> match when an opposing Candidate is speaking, as the noise,
> while muffled in the studio, sounds like a clap of thunder
> outside!

No listening figures had, at this time, been published by Radio
Oxford, although it did seem unlikely that they had any significant
numbers of listeners in the Colleges.

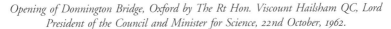

*Opening of Donnington Bridge, Oxford by The Rt Hon. Viscount Hailsham QC, Lord
President of the Council and Minister for Science, 22nd October, 1962.*

Robert Maxwell, MC MP and the Directors of Pergamon Press Limited requested the pleasure of my company at a ceremony at Headington Hill Hall, Oxford, at 4 p.m. on Friday, 15 July 1966, on the occasion of the presentation of The Queen's Award to industry 1966 by Colonel John Thomson, TD, Lord Lieutenant of Oxfordshire on behalf of Her Majesty The Queen.

I was Vice Chairman of the Traffic Committee. This was one of the major committees covering, as it did, all traffic regulations, including parking and traffic lights.

New buses were always inspected by the Committee before being put on service. Sometimes we considered the steps were too high or the entrances were wrong. A number were sent back for alterations, or cancelled altogether.

While on the City Council I was invited to the Boar's Head Ceremony at the Queen's College. My son accompanied me and we were given printed information about the ceremony:

Myself on motorcycle in simulated road scene. I was then Vice Chairman of the Traffic Committee. Lady McDougall is seen with Police Cadets.
Reproduced by courtesy of the Oxford Mail.

Stage coach used for campaigning for the successful election of the candidate in 1938. Myself in front next to driver.

The Boar's Head Ceremony, which has been celebrated in the College for more than five hundred years, begins with half an hour's singing of carols by the choir from the gallery above the Hall.

When the clock strikes the hour of seven, the doors of the Hall are opened (at this point those attending the ceremony are asked to stand), and the trumpet is sounded, as it is every night, first in the Front Quad and again in the back Quad, to summon the Provost and Fellows to dinner. They enter in procession and take their places at the High Table.

Then the Boar's head procession itself enters the Hall, headed by a cantor. Cantor and choir sing the College's traditional carol as they advance.

The Boar's Head, borne on a silver dish and carried by three cooks, is placed on the table in front of the Provost. The orange from the mouth is given to the singer, and the decorated leaves surrounding it are distributed first to the choir and then to any visitors attending the ceremony who wish to have them.

Christmas Card from the Mayor and Mayoress of Oxford Alderman and Mrs Lionel Harrison, 1961, showing view of Oxford from Hinksey Hill. Alderman Harrison was the last Mayor of Oxford.

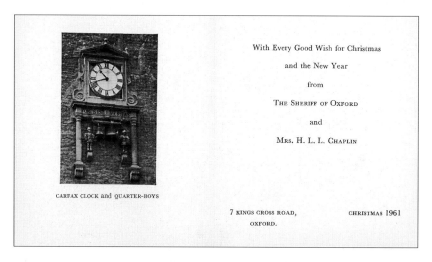

Christmas Card showing Carfax Clock and Quarter-Boys from the Sheriff of Oxford and Mrs H. L. L. Chaplin, 1961.

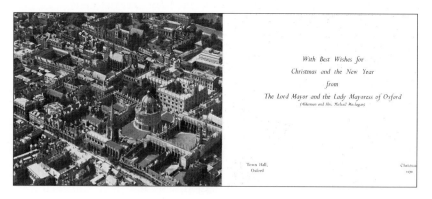

Christmas Card from the Lord Mayor and Mayoress of Oxford, Alderman and Mrs Michael Maclagan, 1970. View of central Oxford, North of High Street.

Women's Gas Federation

I JOINED the inaugural meeting of the Oxford Branch at the Gas Showroom in Oxford. It went off to a wonderful start and at the conclusion of the first meeting, 84 members had enrolled and paid their subscriptions. In one year we had over 100 members. Meals were cooked at the meeting at the Gas Showroom. It was therefore shown how versatile gas can be.

Then we had to move from the Gas Showroom and find other accommodation. This was not easy to find in the centre of the city, but finally we found a small church hall in Cornmarket Street. From then on we gradually began to lose members until finally our membership fell from 100 to between 30 to 40.

Much was done to keep it going and a notice appeared in the Press and Gas Showrooms, which was an open invitation to meet Margaret Powell. Her book *Service below Stairs* is well known. She was a first-class speaker. It was a marvellous afternoon held at the Randolph Hotel, with tea to follow. About 200 people attended, but the membership increased by only five.

After this it was decided nothing further could be done and so after its thirty years in existence, the Committee agreed that the Oxford Branch should close down. Members were welcomed by the Witney Branch which has always been well organised, with good officers and Committee, and always a first class Fixture List.

During the time I was on the Oxford Branch I was elected a Council member. When elected I automatically ceased to be a member of the Branch. As a Council member I soon found the work involved a terrific amount of travelling.

Committees were mostly held in London at the Institution of Gas Engineers, whose premises were then in Grosvenor Crescent,

Members of the Women's Gas Federation being shown the City Plate at the Town Hall by the City Mace Bearer, Leslie Boddy.

London. They started at 9.30 a.m. with a break for lunch and continued until about 3 p.m. Because of the early start it meant travelling the day before and staying the night at an hotel. Here we met other Council members from different parts of the country. Four of us always stayed at the Green Park Hotel, Piccadilly. The day before headquarters usually arranged some kind of visit for us and this saved being alone in London. We visited the Science Museum and Watson House where, at the end of our tour, we were invited to either lunch or dinner.

One of the first Committee meetings I attended in London included a training session for a radio interview. Each member was interviewed separately in a special room on a question and answer basis. Later in the afternoon it was recorded back with general comments from the interviewer. This was useful if asked to give a radio talk.

Apart from this our work involved visiting branches, and co-ordinating meetings at Reading. Twice a year a Council member

MINISTRY OF POWER

ESTABLISHMENTS DIVISION

Thames House South, Millbank, LONDON S.W.1

Telephone: Abbey 7000

Our reference: ESTAB. 37/238/A3

16th November, 1967

Your reference:

PERSONAL

Dear Madam,

I have to inform you that the Minister of Power has appointed you, under Section 9(2)(a) of the Gas Act, 1948, and the Gas (Consultative Council) Regulations, 1949, to be a member of the Consultative Council for the area of the Southern Gas Board, subject to the provisions of the said Act and Regulations.

No salary is payable to members and the appointment, which will be for a period of two years from 15th November 1967, carries no right to pension or gratuity on its termination. You will, however, be entitled to claim reimbursement of reasonable travelling and out-of-pocket expenses incurred directly on the business of the Council; further details can be obtained from the Secretary of the Council.

A list of the Chairman and members of the Consultative Council is attached for your information.

I am, Madam,
Your obedient Servant,

Councillor Mrs. A.F. Wood,
232 Headington Road,
OXFORD.

(W. E. R. Chamberlain)

VAC

Letter dated 16th November 1967 confirming my appointment as a member of the Consultative Council for the area of the Southern Gas Board.

met the Branch Liaison Officer and the Regional Home Service Adviser at Southampton. Here we looked at the Region as a whole.

Apart from this a Council member was elected to represent the Council on such organisations as WRVS, the National Council of Women and ROSPA. I was asked to represent the Council on ROSPA. A written report had then to be drafted to each Council member for discussion at our Committee meetings.

But one of most memorable occasions was when all the Council members received an invitation from our President, Lady Howe, to a cocktail party at 11 Downing Street. On this occasion four of us were staying at the Green Park Hotel and we all felt very important when the taxi arrived. When we asked the driver to take us to 11 Downing Street, his reply was, 'You're pulling my leg, try again.' At last we convinced him and off we went.

The policeman smiled as we produced our invitation cards and we were allowed to enter Downing Street and be driven to No. 11. Here we were met by a man servant who examined our handbags, 'Just to make sure,' he said. We then proceeded upstairs where Lady Howe was greeting her guests.

We sat around a long polished table thinking of the number of important people who had sat round the same table when discussing affairs of the State. One got the impression that the State room where the party was held was very much a business room. Two very important padlocked cases stood alongside one wall and a marble fireplace was overhung by a gilt framed mirror. There were also pictures of various views. Apart from a glass chandelier that hung from the ceiling, there was little relief.

When the meeting was nearly over Sir, now Lord Geoffrey Howe, put his head round the door, and with a charming smile, asked if we were ready for tea. If so he would go and put the kettle on, and he meant it. Shortly after he reappeared, teapot in hand, accompanied by his two daughters, who waited on us at tea. It was a delightful occasion, and a most interesting and

Being presented with a bouquet by the Witney Branch of the Women's Gas Federation and Young Homemakers. The inscription on the right headed Literacy reads: If you educate a man you educate a person, but if you educate a woman you educate a family.

enjoyable evening. We were only sorry when a taxi was called to take us back to the hotel.

Once a year, Lady Howe invited us to a cocktail party and this was always held in the Gas premises in Grosvenor Crescent. It was always a lovely occasion.

National Savings

DURING World War II street and village groups were first established in 1942. National Savings encouraged the public to save for the benefit of the individual and also for the Country.

It was at its peak in 1945 when it was indicated that there were 19,000 Groups selling National Savings Stamps and Certificates from door to door.

After the war it was decided that the National Savings Stamp should continue to be sold. It could be used for saving for Radio and Television licenses and also for Gas, Electricity, Rates and holidays. Later, the National Savings Oxfordshire and North Berkshire Committee was set up.

I was on the City Council at the time and being Vice Chairman of the National Savings Committee, I was invited to sit on the local Committee as District Representative on the Regional Street, Village and Social Committee. Mr Burton was Commissioner for the Southern Region and Mr Preece-James was the local District Commissioner.

In 1973 I attended the Southern Regional Conference when I was asked to act as Secretary to the Meeting. I also gave the Sectional Report to the Main Conference. At that time it was stated that 19 per cent of the population had money invested in Building Societies, 23 per cent in Bank Deposit Accounts and 8 per cent in Unit Trusts, Stocks and Shares, or Local Authority Securities. Thirty-one per cent of the population had no savings at all and only 8 per cent of personal disposable income was saved. This compared with 14–16 per cent in most European countries.

I helped with their Community Month and found it most interesting. We had a special stall in the covered market which

The National Savings indicator attached to Carfax Tower. The National Savings Committee Organisation was set up in March 1916 to promote savings to assist in the war effort. It continued in being in war and peace playing an increasingly important part in the finances of the nation and in the development of a sense of financial responsibility in the individual. The organisation was modified and new securities were introduced to meet changing conditions. In September 1977 the Government withdrew the Civil Service support staff from the Voluntary Movement, which then virtually ceased to exist.

was manned by volunteers. There were special advertisements in the Press and Post Office vans carried special posters. Twenty thousand bookmarks were issued to the City and County Libraries. It was a great success.

We finished with a garden party and a special Community Cake. There was also the Duke of Edinburgh's Award Scheme. This was held in a Hall in New Inn Hall Street. Children came of their own free will according to which session they preferred. I spoke on the Aims and Ideals of the National Savings Movement and my class was attended by twelve children. Later, I was elected to the Regional Street and Village Groups. The meetings were usually held in Reading and covered Representatives from all over the Region. As Representatives it was our duty to our local Savings Committee to put forward any plans from Committee throughout their District.

There were also Annual Conferences. These were usually held at seaside resorts. I remember the very last one was held at Ryde on the Isle of Wight. When I was shown to my hotel room I had ten beds to choose from. I chose the middle one. Next morning, when the maid brought my early cup of tea, she had to walk nearly the length of the room before finding me. All the other beds were still empty. I thought this was funny, but I was then told there was a misunderstanding between National Savings and the proprietor of the hotel. The next night I was moved into a nice single room.

It was at this Conference we heard that the Government was considering terminating the sale of the Savings Stamp in 1976. This I think ended one of the most difficult jobs in the savings movement, especially for those people who were, after all, the keystone of the Street, Village and Social Organisation. In January 1976 a meeting of the Oxfordshire Educational Savings Committee was held.

At the meeting it was suggested that all street group workers who were interested might continue in National Savings helping

Myself being awarded the British Empire medal by Sir John Anstey, President and Chairman, National Savings Committee.

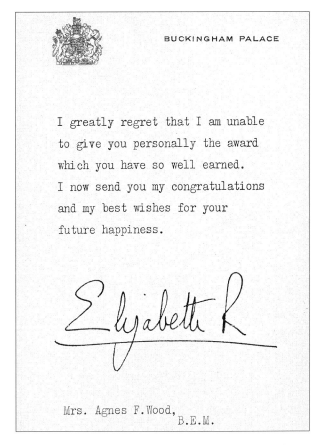

BUCKINGHAM PALACE

I greatly regret that I am unable
to give you personally the award
which you have so well earned.
I now send you my congratulations
and my best wishes for your
future happiness.

Elizabeth R

Mrs. Agnes F.Wood, B.E.M.

*Note from her
Majesty the Queen.*

local schools in the running of local school savings banks. At that time there were approximately 100 schools with stamp groups and these would be lost to the savings movement if no alternative method could be found.

At a subsequent meeting of this Committee on 3 May 1976 at Westminster College, I reported on the position to see whether or not the Street Group secretaries were in agreement with the proposal. The Chief Education Officer endorsed the suggestion and Oxfordshire teachers were told that back-up support would be given.

In December 1976 I received a letter from 10 Downing Street. Inside was a letter marked 'In Confidence' and informing me that The Queen had been graciously pleased to approve the Prime

Group, Oxford National Savings. Oxford Town Hall.

Minister's recommendation that the British Empire Medal be awarded to me.

The award was announced in the New Year Honours List. In January 1977 I received a letter from the President and Chairman of the National Savings Committee, Sir John Anstey, informing me that he would present the Medal on behalf of Her Majesty at a ceremony at the Headquarters, Alexandra House, Kingsway, on the morning of Wednesday, 23 March 1977. I also received a note from The Queen at Buckingham Palace, signed Elizabeth R.

This said 'I greatly regret that I am unable to give you personally the award you have so well earned. I now send you my congratulations and my best wishes for your future happiness'.

My son accompanied me. There were five of us to receive the British Empire Medal. After the presentation of the British Empire Medals, lunch was provided at the Waldorf Hotel, Aldwych. After lunch we went by taxi to visit St Paul's Cathedral where a Chapel of the Order of the British Empire Medal is open to 3.30 p.m. each weekday. I was later invited to a Service of Dedication which took place in St Paul's Cathedral on Wednesday, 4 May 1977 at

2.30 p.m. This was headed 'The Most Excellent Order of the British Empire.'

At 2.15 the Lord Mayor, with his Officers, arrived at the West Door to be received by the Dean and Chapter with the Bishop of London. He then moved to the foot of the steps to await the arrival of Her Royal Highness Princess Alice, Duchess of Gloucester, and His Royal Highness the Duke of Edinburgh.

The band of the Irish Guards played voluntaries before and after the Service. The Service ended with a fanfare leading into the National Anthem, followed by the Blessing.

Eric Preece-James resigned in 1972 as the local National Savings District Commissioner and there was a farewell party in the Lord Mayor's Parlour.

He read the following verse:

> I remember, I remember, the folk in Oxford City
> That they're not known to many more
> I vow it is a pity
> Loyal, steadfast and all dark blue
> Just knowing them, brings out the best in you
> Clarice, Florence, and that great stalwart John,
> Gordon, Bill, Maud and Ron
> So many members, too many to mention
> to whose excellent service I could draw attention
> Their list of achievements is splendid to see
> And they are brilliantly led by dear G.E.C.
>
> Nor do I omit to remember
> The Lord Mayor and friends of the Council Chamber,
> And Mr Rook, loyal and true
> For advice and counsel, I give thanks to you
> And the General Manager and staff of the T.S.B.
> Always and ever an inspiration to me.
>
> In schools, Mr John Garne, cleverly sets the pace
> And young National Savers, fly all over the place,
> The year has gone so fast, we know not where it went
> But at the end, our membership's up by 25 per cent

Invitation to tea on the occasion of my 90th birthday.

And our target, 30 million in one year round
We've reached it and passed it by five million pound.

Great City of Oxford with tradition and spire,
Sometimes we've bedecked you in Savings attire,
Our flags have flown from many a mast,
Yes, even over the G.P.O. at last
Oh so many good things there are to remember
To mention them all it would take till December.

And now we are gathered in Oxford Town Hall
In the Lord Mayor's Parlour where men walk tall,
Not to say Goodbye but just a fond adieu
Because I'm not going to be so very far from you,
And wherever we meet and Oxford friends I see
I'll remember your kindness to my wife and to me.

THE END